TRANSACTIONS

AMERICAN PHILOSOPHICAL SOCIETY

HELD AT PHILADELPHIA

FOR PROMOTING USEFUL KNOWLEDGE

VOLUME 69, PART 4 · 1979

The Origins of Calvin's Theology of Music: 1536–1543

CHARLES GARSIDE, JR.

PROFESSOR OF HISTORY, RICE UNIVERSITY

THE AMERICAN PHILOSOPHICAL SOCIETY

INDEPENDENCE SQUARE: PHILADELPHIA

August, 1979

PUBLICATIONS

OF

The American Philosophical Society

The publications of the American Philosophical Society consist of PRO-CEEDINGS, TRANSACTIONS, MEMOIRS, and YEAR BOOK.

THE PROCEEDINGS contains papers which have been read before the Society in addition to other papers which have been accepted for publication by the Committee on Publications. In accordance with the present policy one volume is issued each year, consisting of six bimonthly numbers, and the price is $10.00 net per volume.

THE TRANSACTIONS, the oldest scholarly journal in America, was started in 1769 and is quarto size. In accordance with the present policy each annual volume is a collection of monographs, each issued as a part. The current annual subscription price is $25.00 net per volume. Individual copies of the TRANSACTIONS are offered for sale.

Each volume of the MEMOIRS is published as a book. The titles cover the various fields of learning; most of the recent volumes have been historical. The price of each volume is determined by its size and character, but subscribers are offered a twenty per cent discount.

The YEAR BOOK is of considerable interest to scholars because of the reports on grants for research and to libraries for this reason and because of the section dealing with the acquisitions of the Library. In addition it contains the Charter and Laws, and lists of members, and reports of committees and meetings. The YEAR BOOK is published about April 1 for the preceding calendar year. The current price is $5.00.

An author desiring to submit a manuscript for publication should send it to the Editor, George W. Corner, American Philosophical Society, 104 South Fifth Street, Philadelphia, Pa. 19106.

TRANSACTIONS OF THE

AMERICAN PHILOSOPHICAL SOCIETY

HELD AT PHILADELPHIA

FOR PROMOTING USEFUL KNOWLEDGE

VOLUME 69, PART 4 · 1979

The Origins of Calvin's Theology of Music: 1536–1543

CHARLES GARSIDE, JR.

PROFESSOR OF HISTORY, RICE UNIVERSITY

THE AMERICAN PHILOSOPHICAL SOCIETY

INDEPENDENCE SQUARE: PHILADELPHIA

August, 1979

Library of Congress Catalog
Card Number 78-73171
International Standard Book Number 0-87169-694-0
US ISSN 0065-9746

IN MEMORIAM

Roy Dickinson Welch 1885–1951

and

Sylvia Spencer Welch 1893–1973

HOMAGIUM AUCTORIS

ACKNOWLEDGMENTS

A preliminary version of this essay was read in St. Louis on October 30, 1976, before a joint session of the American Society for Reformation Research and the American Academy of Religion. I wish to thank Professor Joyce Irwin of the University of Georgia and Professor Bartlett R. Butler of Luther College for their perceptive comments on that occasion. To the then president of the society, Professor Miriam U. Chrisman, I am greatly indebted for her enthusiastic insistence that I prepare the paper for publication.

I am under a particular obligation to Professor Ford Lewis Battles of the Pittsburgh Theological Seminary. He read an intermediate draft with painstaking care, and the final version has benefited not simply from his unrivaled learning, but from his generous encouragement as well.

At Rice University, Professors Deborah H. Nelson and Susan L. Clark in the Departments of French and German respectively, have freely come to my aid when I have encountered problems in translating Calvin and Bucer, while in the Department of History my colleague Professor Albert Van Helden provided indispensable assistance with the Dutch. I have also to thank Mr. James Mooney and Ms. Kathleen Much Murfin for their meticulous readings of the typescript. For encouragement at a critical moment to bring the work to completion, especial thanks must go to Professor David L. Minter.

I have had to rely more and more heavily for my research on interlibrary loans, and I am much indebted to the efficiency and expertise of the staff of the Fondren Library in procuring books and articles for me, as well as to the many libraries which loaned them. For the skill and exemplary patience in typing more drafts of text and footnotes than I care to recall, I tender special thanks to Ms. Madelyne Brown and Mrs. Linda Quaidy.

Finally I acknowledge with gratitude again the receipt of generous grants-in-aid from the American Philosophical Society and the American Council of Learned Societies which have enabled me to pursue my research on Calvin.

THE ORIGINS OF CALVIN'S THEOLOGY OF MUSIC: 1536-1543

CHARLES GARSIDE, JR.

CONTENTS

I. INTRODUCTION

The singing of psalms was one of the incontestably distinguishing marks of Calvinist culture in Europe and America in the sixteenth and seventeenth centuries. There is no lack of evidence for this phenomenon from contemporary sources: letters, diaries, local chronicles, histories, polemical tracts, martyrologies, written records of all varieties, to say nothing of the numerous editions of the psalters,[1] attest amply and eloquently to the fact that the "Calvinists were convinced that they could legitimately appropriate the psalms to themselves . . . the psalms were *their* songs which they sang as the elect people of God in a covenant relationship with Him."[2] There has been, too, no lack of scholarly investigation of this reformed psalmody. The history of the Huguenot Psalter was first broadly surveyed in 1872 by Félix Bovet from a literary and ecclesiastical point of view; by his own admission he was incompetent to discuss the music.[3]

The lacuna was filled in 1878–1879 with the publication of Orentin Douen's two huge volumes on Clément Marot which Bovet hoped would leave nothing to be desired.[4] Subsequent decades of increasingly sophisticated research proved him wrong; many of Douen's conclusions have either been wholly superseded or put to radical question. The unanticipated complexity of the poetic as well as the musical problems encountered has been recognized to such a degree that in 1962, in the introduction to his critical edition of the Psalter, Pierre Pidoux could assert that despite almost a century of study a synthesis of the phenomenon in its entirety was still not possible.[5] The caution notwithstanding, lineaments of exceptional durability for just such a synthesis were established shortly thereafter by Walter Blankenburg.[6]

What has been lacking, however, ever since the appearance of Bovet's survey, is comparable scholarly examination of Calvin's role in the history of the Psalter, not as a musician, which he was not, nor as a poet, to which he made some aspiration,[7] but as a

---

[1] Within three years of the publication in 1562 of the Genevan Psalter in its completed form, "not less than 63 recorded editions were published, undoubtedly a unique event in the history of Protestant hymnals." Walter Blankenburg in Friedrich Blume, *Protestant Church Music, A History* (New York, W. W. Norton and Company, Inc., 1974) Part V, "Church Music in Reformed Europe," pp. 509–590 at pp. 518–519; hereafter cited as Blankenburg, *Church Music*.

[2] W. Stanford Reid, "The Battle Hymns of the Lord: Calvinist Psalmody of the Sixteenth Century," *Sixteenth Century Essays and Studies*, edited by Carl S. Meyer (Saint Louis, Missouri, The Foundation for Reformation Research, 1971) 2: pp. 36–54 at pp. 43–44.

[3] Félix Bovet, *Histoire du psautier des églises réformées* (Neuchatel, Librairie Générale de J. Sandoz, 1872), pp. ix-x: "j 'ai dû me borner à l'histoire littéraire et ecclésiastique de nos psaumes et laisser presque sans y toucher un côté très-important de cette histoire: je veux parler de la musique, pour

laquelle j'étais absolument incompétent. Cette face du sujet sera traitée sans doute, d'une manière qui ne laissera rien à désirer, par M. Douën qui s'occupe, me dit-on, de l'histoire du Psautier."

[4] Orentin Douen, *Clément Marot et le psautier huguenot* (Paris, Imprimerie Nationale, 1878–1879).

[5] Pierre Pidoux, *Le Psautier Huguenot du XVIᵉ Siècle. Mélodies et Documents,* two volumes (Bâle, Édition Baerenreiter, 1962), I, p. V: ". . . nous devons dire notre conviction que l'heure des travaux de synthèse n'a pas encore sonné." The melodies are published in volume one, hereafter cited as Pidoux, *Mélodies*. Volume two consists of an invaluable collection of all presently known literary documents, printed or archival, relevant to the history of the Psalter, arranged chronologically under successive years from 1537 to 1598; hereafter cited as Pidoux, *Documents*. Samuel Jan Lenselink, *Les Psaumes de Clément Marot* (Assen, Van Gorcum and Comp. N. V., 1969), although independently published, actually constitutes volume three of the critical edition of the Huguenot Psalter. It contains (1) a critical edition of the oldest text with all manuscript variants as well as those editions up to 1543, and (2) the definitive text of 1562. A similar edition by Pierre Pidoux of the Psalms of Théodore de Bèze will constitute volume four.

[6] See *supra*, n. 1.

[7] See Calvin to Conrad Hubert, May 19, 1557: Ad poeticen natura satis eram propensus: sed ea valere iussa, ab annis viginti quinque nihil composui, nisi quod Wormaciae exemplo Philippi et Sturmii adductus sum, ut carmen illud quod legisti per lusum scriberem. *Ioannis Calvini Opera Quae Supersunt Omnia,* edited by W. Baum, E. Cunitz, and E. Reuss (Brunswick, C. A. Schwetschke and Sons, 1863–1900), **XVI**, No. 2632, p. 488; hereafter cited as *OC* with volume number in Roman numerals. The *carmen* to which Calvin alludes is his "Epinicion Christo Cantatum," *OC* **V**, pp. 421–428. Cf. Émile Doumergue, *Jean Calvin, les hommes et*

theologian. So generous was Bovet's frame of reference, despite the brevity of his book, that Calvin was but slightly mentioned.[8] Douen focused in meticulous detail on the origins of the Psalter in the sixteenth century, but was unremittingly hostile to the reformer, denouncing him as an "enemy of all pleasure and of all distraction, even of the arts and of music."[9] Émile Doumergue tried to correct this influential and tenacious judgment, notably in an emotionally charged lecture of 1902, but failed, precisely because for the most part he drew attention to the extensive use to which the Huguenots put the psalms after they had been set to music rather than to Calvin's own understanding of why this should have been done in the first place. "Such, gentlemen," he exclaimed, "is the art, the theory of which Calvin laid down, and such is the song of which Calvin was the inspirer and the propagator. This is what Calvin thought of music, and did for music."[10] Doumergue had limned something of the latter; the former, however, he virtually ignored.

Finally in 1932 Léon Wencelius addressed himself to an examination of Calvin and *all* the arts—the first, and thus far the only scholar to do so on a systematic and thoroughly comprehensive scale.[11] His long exposition of the reformer's views on music was entitled, appropriately, "Musique et chant sacré,"[12] for, as Wencelius clearly realized, Calvin very rarely, if indeed ever, wrote about music independently of its relationship specifically to public communal worship or the praise of God in general. His point of view was never that of the aesthetician; it was, to the contrary, always that of the theologian, and although Wencelius did not use the phrase, what Calvin had to say about the art can therefore be understood and designated only as a theology of music.

Much of the analysis to which Wencelius put the texts is penetrating and of permanent value, but he was so little concerned with context and chronology that the question of the origins and development of Calvin's attitude toward music received no attention. Since 1932 only two studies on the subject have appeared which are of comparable value, Walter Blankenburg's article on Calvin written for *Die Musik in Geschichte und Gegenwart* (1952),[13] and the section devoted to Calvin in the chapter on the "Theologische Grundlagen der Musik" which Oskar Söhngen contributed to *Leiturgia,* published in 1961.[14] Against both, however, as against Wencelius, the same objection must be leveled. Neither is historical in the essential sense of tracing ideas through time. Calvin's earliest surviving references to music are to be found in the *Institution* of 1536; in 1543 he enlarged the preface to the Genevan Psalter with the longest single passage on the subject ever to come from his pen. Initially his reserve about the value of admitting music to worship was such that on the basis of what he published in 1536 the possibility of a Calvinist liturgy

les choses de son temps (Geneva, Slatkine Reprints, 1969), **2**, Appendice No. VI, "Calvin Poète," pp. 742–743; hereafter cited as Doumergue, *Calvin.* For Calvin's versions of the Psalms, see *infra,* ns. 80 and 81.

[8] Bovet, *op. cit.,* pp. 13–18.

[9] Douen, *op. cit.,* **I**, p. 377: ". . . ennemi de tout plaisir et de toute distraction, même des arts et de la musique; . . ." The entire paragraph is typical of his animosity.

[10] Émile Doumergue, "Music in the Work of Calvin," *The Princeton Theological Review* 7, No. 4 (October, 1909): pp. 529–552 at p. 547. The essay is a translation of "La musique dans l'oeuvre de Calvin," the first of three public lectures by Doumergue published under the title *L'art et le sentiment dans l'oeuvre de Calvin* (Geneva, Slatkine Reprints, 1970), pp. 7–30. The English translation has been reprinted in *The Banner of Truth* **160** (January, 1977): pp. 6–10; **161** (February, 1977): pp. 7–17.

[11] Léon Wencelius, *L'esthétique de Calvin* (Paris, Société d' édition "Les Belles Lettres," 1938). He had in fact been preceded, as he himself acknowledged (p. 98), by the inaugural dissertation of Marta Grau, *Calvins Stellung zur Kunst* (Wurzburg, Buchdruckerei Franz Staudenraus, 1917), but the essay is of no consequence. Its superficiality may best be gauged by the fact that in a total of seventy-six pages Grau treats not only Calvin's attitude toward ecclesiastical art and music, but rhetoric, literature, theater, and even antiquity as well. The pages devoted to music (21–35; 46–47) consist for the most part of quotations from Calvin without critical analysis.

[12] Wencelius, *op. cit.,* pp. 250–303 in all; only pp. 250–280, however, are devoted to Calvin's ideas on music.

[13] Walter Blankenburg, "Calvin," *Die Musik in Geschichte und Gegenwart* (Kassel und Basel, Bärenreiter-Verlag, 1952) **2**: cols. 653–666; hereafter cited as Blankenburg, *Calvin.* The article, remarkable in itself for its consistently accurate information and sympathetic insight, is also unique. There is no equivalent in any other musical dictionary or encyclopedia. With respect to Calvin the English reader is in this regard particularly disadvantaged. *Grove's Dictionary of Music and Musicians,* for example, now in its fifth edition (London, Macmillan and Co., Ltd., 1954), under Calvin (**2**: p. 24) simply refers the reader to the article on Bourgeois in which nothing is to be found on the Reformer's ideas about, or attitude toward, music. Although there are brief entries in *The Oxford Companion to Music* (10th Edition, London, Oxford University Press, 1970, p. 149) and *The Concise Oxford Dictionary of Music* (2nd Edition, London, Oxford University Press, 1969, p. 88), in neither is Calvin's significance for the history of music explained.

[14] Oskar Söhngen, "Theologische Grundlagen der Kirchenmusik," *Leiturgia: Handbuch des evangelischen Gottesdienstes,* IV, *Die Musik des evangelischen Gottesdienstes* (Kassel, Johannes Stauda-Verlag, 1961), pp. 1–267 at Part III, "Calvin," pp. 38–62; hereafter cited as Söhngen, *Calvin.* Separate reference must be made to H. Hasper, *Calvijns beginsel voor de zang in de eredienst. Verklaard uit de Heilige Schrift en uit de geschiedenis der kerk. Een kerkhistorisch en hymnologisch onderzoek,* Deel I (The Hague, Martinus Nijhoff, 1955). It is an enormous book (774 pages), written in difficult Dutch, self-indulgent with regard to its stupefying mass of detail, and not infrequently polemical in tone. There are summaries at the end respectively in Dutch, French, German, and English (pp. 747–774). Despite its formidable bulk and erudition, even the chapters most closely related to Calvin, above all "Calvijn en de musiek" (pp. 401–411) proved of little assistance in my effort to understand the early development of Calvin's thinking about music; hereafter cited as Hasper, *Calvijns beginsel.*

employing music to any considerable degree seemed at best remote. Seven years later, however, he revealed himself as a determined, although by no means uncritical, advocate of psalmody and the superintending editor as well of what eventually would be one of the most influential psalters ever created for Christian worship.[15] What was responsible for this change in opinion? When did it occur? How did Calvin's thinking on the subject develop? To whom may it have been indebted? Notwithstanding the magnitude of his musical achievement as much in his editorial labors as in his theological formulations, these questions have been raised only incidentally or occasionally; never have they received the careful scrutiny which they deserve. The present essay therefore endeavors to answer them. By eliminating from consideration all his later statements on music, and examining as closely as possible only the evidence available from 1536 to June 10, 1543, when he completed the preface to the Genevan Psalter, it seeks to penetrate Calvin's mind during these years and to reconstruct the creative process by which he laid the foundations for his theology of music.

II.　THE POINT OF ORIGIN

On January 16, 1537, Calvin laid before the council certain *Articles* for the organization of the church and its worship in Geneva.[16] No more than six months earlier he had acceded to Farel's demand to assist him in reforming the city, and Geneva had made its

official decision "to live according to the Gospel and the Word of God"[17] only on May 21 of the preceding year. There had been since then much "trouble and confusion," the people were still "ignorant," and "good order" could not possibly be effected in a single stroke.[18] To that end, however, so Calvin argued, a major step forward would be taken by means of the following: initiating the discipline of excommunication to preserve the integrity of the church with respect above all to the Lord's Supper; introducing the singing of psalms into public worship; instructing children in evangelical doctrine to maintain its continuity and purity; and drafting marriage ordinances. These were the first essentials, without which the new church could be neither "well ordered" nor "regulated." They were, moreover, derived "from the holy Word of the Gospel."[20] On this Calvin almost immediately insisted, and in concluding the document he was at pains to emphasize again that the four proposals were not of his invention, but "truly from the Word of God."[21] Given, then, this double context— that, on the one hand, of the imperative for civil and ecclesiastical order, and on the other, of the imperative for conforming as closely as possible to Scriptural practice in the establishment of this order—Calvin's first sentence on music assumes a significance insufficiently acknowledged:[22]

Furthermore it is a thing most expedient for the edification of the church to sing some psalms [23] in the form of

---

[15] See, for instance, Blankenburg, *Church Music,* p. 530: "Never again, at any time or place in the history of Protestant hymnals based on Calvin's principles, would there be a treasury of poems and songs, of sheer ecumenical significance, equal to the Genevan Psalter in unity, durability, and, eventually, wide dissemination."

[16] *Articles concernant l'organisation de l'église et du culte a Genève, proposés au conseil par les ministres,* January 16, 1537, *OC* **X**[1]: pp. 5–14. See also *Correspondence des réformateurs dans les pays de langue française,* edited by Aimé-Louis Herminjard (Nieuwkoop, B. DeGraaf, 1965–1966), **IV,** No. 602, pp. 154–166; hereafter cited as Herminjard, and *Joannis Calvini Opera Selecta,* edited by Peter Barth (Munich, Christian Kaiser, 1926), 1, pp. 369–377 from which the present translation has been made; hereafter cited as *OS* with volume number in Arabic numerals. The passages devoted to music are excerpted and reproduced in Pidoux, *Documents,* p. 1. Unless otherwise indicated, all translations are my own. There is a complete and reliable English translation by J. K. S. Reid in *Calvin: Theological Treatises, The Library of Christian Classics* (Philadelphia, The Westminster Press, 1954) 22: pp. 48–55.

On the two problems of the disputed authorship of the document between Farel and Calvin, and the date of its composition see Williston Walker, *John Calvin, The Organizer of Reformed Protestantism: 1509–1564* (New York, G. P. Putnam's Sons, 1909), pp. 184–185 and the literature cited. In accepting Calvin's sole authorship I follow Walker. See also more recently Eugène Choisy, "Farel A Genève avec Calvin, De 1536 A 1538," *Guillaume Farel, 1489–1565* (Neuchatel/ Paris, Éditions Delachaux et Niestlé, 1930), pp. 348–361 at p. 352.

[17] *OC* **XXI:** p. 201.

[18] For words and phrases in quotation marks, see *OC* **X**[1]: p. 7; *OS* 1: p. 370.

[19] *OC* **X**[1]: pp. 5–6; *OS* 1: p. 369.

[20] *OC* **X**[1]: p. 7; *OS* 1: p. 370.

[21] *OC* **X**[1]: p. 14; *OS* 1: p. 376.

[22] Walker, *op. cit.,* p. 192, for instance, does not even consider the singing of psalms to be one of Calvin's "principal recommendations"; see also Choisy, *op. cit.,* p. 353. Amédée Roget, *Histoire du peuple de Genève depuis la Réforme jusqu'à l'Escalade* (Genève, John Jullien), 1 (1870): pp. 15–20, acknowledges the critical importance of the *Articles* and subjects them to "un examen minutieux," but without once mentioning psalmody. Doumergue in his analysis of the document (*Calvin,* 2: pp. 219–227) omits discussion of the musical recommendation, reserving this for a later chapter (pp. 505–524). Along among earlier biographers, Hugh Y. Reyburn, *John Calvin. His Life, Letters, and Work* (London, Hodder and Stoughton, 1914), pp. 63–64, puts Calvin's request for congregational psalmody in its immediate historical context. He is followed in this most recently by T. H. L. Parker, *John Calvin: A Biography* (Philadelphia, The Westminster Press, 1975), p. 63. Elsewhere Parker explicitly states, the first to my knowledge to do so, that "one of the four foundations for the reform of the Church was congregational singing" (p. 87).

[23] What Calvin meant by "pseaumes" poses a problem. Herminjard, **IV,** No. 602, p. 163 n. 15, suggests that at this time the word meant generally spiritual songs, "cantiques," such as the ones published at Neuchâtel in 1533 (*cf.* Herminjard, **II,** No. 384, p. 431 n. 14 and p. 489). See also Théophile Dufour, *Notice bibliographique sur le Catéchisme et la Confession de Foi de Calvin (1537) et sur les autres livres imprimés à Genève et à Neuchâtel dans les premiers temps de la*

public prayers by which one prays to God or sings His praises so that the hearts of all may be aroused and stimulated to make similar prayers and to render similar praises and thanks to God with a common love.[24]

The singing of psalms was not an indifferent matter. To the contrary, it was *essential* for public worship. Moreover, in Calvin's order of priorities for the new church, it was second only to the need for establishing excommunication. Here, accordingly, in the *Articles* of 1537, is the point of origin for his theology of music.

III. THE *INSTITUTION* OF 1536

The decisiveness of the statement on psalmody is heightened by a close reading of the *Institution* of 1536. In it the third chapter was devoted to prayer. Throughout his general considerations on the subject preceding the exposition of the Lord's Prayer, Calvin was demonstrably more concerned for private as opposed to public prayer, above all, perhaps, in his endeavor to analyze the proper interior disposition of the individual when praying. He must strive to comply with Saint Paul's injunction to "pray without

ceasing," to achieve a "constancy in prayer" having "nothing to do with the public prayers of the church."[25] Even though for the latter "temples" have been set aside, "we ourselves," Calvin argued, "are the true temples of God," and we should therefore, if we "wish to pray in God's temple, pray in ourselves."[26] Commenting briefly on Matthew 6:6, Christ's injunction to withdrawal and secrecy was judged by Calvin "the best rule for prayer,"[27] and the essence of prayer was defined as "an emotion of the heart within."[28] Concluding that prayer was "principally lodged in the heart,"[29] Calvin immediately thereafter wrote as follows: "From this, moreover, it is fully evident that unless voice and song [*cantum*], if interposed in prayer, spring from deep feeling of heart, neither has any value or profit in the least with God."[30] The introduction of song into the discussion is abrupt and unexpected; it is, in fact, the first reference to music in the *Institution*. To be noted also is the fact that Calvin writes "voice and song," placing voice first, emphasizing thereby that he has been thinking about the silent, private prayer of the individual. To such prayer the addition of the spoken or the sung word is condemned out of hand as being utterly worthless unless either or both are deeply felt, for mere sound "from the tip of the lips and from the throat"[31] is an abuse and a mockery of true prayer.

"Yet," he continues, "we do not here condemn speaking and singing provided they are associated with the heart's affection and serve it."[32] Speaking and singing in private prayer are thus permissible only if they are, quite literally, heartfelt; they must be confined to serving that fundamental emotion. Strictly within the terms of this qualification, speaking and singing may also "exercise the mind in thinking of God and keep it attentive."[33] And, too, Calvin points out,

since the glory of God ought, in a measure, to shine in the several parts of our bodies, it is especially fitting that the tongue has been assigned and destined for this task, both through singing [*canendo*] and through speaking. For it was expressly created to tell and proclaim the praise of God.[34]

The individual, then, while at prayer, may sing and speak, although, as Calvin shortly says, "the tongue is not even necessary for private prayer: the inner feel-

---

réforme (*1533–1540*) (Geneva, Slatkine Reprints, 1970), *passim*, but especially pp. 104–105, 108–110, and 112–113, as well as the extended discussion in Hasper, *Calvijns beginsel*, pp. 444–455. Earlier Hasper insists (p. 431) that in the *Articles* "when Calvin and his colleagues speak to the city magistracy about *the psalms*, they mean by this a well-known ecclesiastical concept. The *PSALMS* meant: everything which was being 'sung' in the church at that time," in other words the whole musical repertoire of the pre-Reformation church. No contemporary evidence is given to support the assertion. That this was truly what Calvin meant, Hasper says further, "cannot be contradicted" (p. 431). As proof (pp. 431–432) he points particularly to the fact that the Strasbourg Psalter of 1539 included material other than the psalms (which it did), and the fact that the title of the Strasbourg Liturgy of 1542 speaks of "Franse Psalmen en liederen," i.e., "pseaulmes et canticques." He concludes accordingly, by virtue of the distinction made between "pseaulmes" and "canticques," that only by 1542 did the word "psalms" mean for Calvin specifically and exclusively the psalms of the Old Testament. The evidence may be read differently, however, for Calvin is nothing if not precise in his use of language. When he spoke of singing the psalms in the *Institutio* of 1536 and the *Articles* of 1537 I am inclined to believe that he meant the psalms, and *nothing else*, especially since versions in French were available. When, therefore, in 1538 he discovered that other songs, "cantiques," were used at Strasbourg, of which he approved, he underscored the inclusion of the additional material in his Strasbourg Psalter (1539) by explicitly entitling it *Aulcuns pseaulmes et cantiques*. Hasper does not seem to recognize that Calvin makes the distinction as early as 1539. The phrase "pseaulmes et canticques francoys" in the Strasbourg Liturgy of 1542 simply repeats the distinction made in the Strasbourg Psalter. The evidence presently available cannot yield a definitive conclusion.

[24] *OC* **X**[1]: p. 6; *OS* 1: p. 369: Dauantage cest vne chose bien expediente a ledification de lesglise de chanter aulcungs pseaumes en forme doraysons publicqs par les quelz on face prieres a Dieu ou que on chante ses louanges affin que les cueurs de tous soyent esmeuz et jncites a former pareilles oraysons et rendre pareilles louanges et graces a Dieu dune mesme affection.

---

[25] John Calvin, *Institution of the Christian Religion*, translated and annotated by Ford Lewis Battles (Atlanta, John Knox Press, 1975), p. 99; hereafter cited as *Institution*. *Cf.* *OC* **I**: p. 87; *OS* 1: p. 102.

[26] *Institution*, p. 99; *OC* **I**: p. 87; *OS* 1: p. 102.

[27] *Institution*, p. 100; *OC* **I**: p. 87, *OS* 1: p. 102.

[28] *Institution*, p. 99; *OC* **I**: p. 87; *OS* 1: p. 102.

[29] *Institution*, p. 100; *OC* **I**, p. 88; *OS* 1, p. 103.

[30] *Ibid.*

[31] *Ibid.*

[32] *Ibid.*

[33] *Ibid.*

[34] *Ibid.*

ing would be enough to arouse itself, so that sometimes the best prayers are silent ones." [35]

What kind of music did Calvin have in mind? The question, important as it is, cannot at present be answered. Collections of spiritual songs for private devotions were of course available,[36] but we do not know definitively whether Calvin knew them, or, if he did, whether he was thinking of any one or ones in particular. He speaks merely of song [*cantum*], and singing [*canendo*]; neither is elaborated. Nor is the fact surprising. Calvin's overriding concern at the time was for the interiority of prayer as over against any external form. His insistence that neither prayer to nor praise of God was of any avail unless it came deeply and truly from the heart is pointed; central to prayer was the inner, inaudible, spiritual state of the individual; speaking and singing, regardless of what sort, were of peripheral importance. "The tongue without the heart is unacceptable to God." [37] If, therefore, in private prayer the heart was rightly disposed, and if words, spoken or sung, were genuinely and consistently subservient to it, their use was not to be condemned. Beyond that minimal assertion he would not go.

That Calvin here pronounces no opinion on the use of song in public prayers is, on the other hand, perplexing. He had completed the *Institution* in Basel, and German versions of the psalms had been enthusiastically sung by congregations there since August of 1526.[38] Calvin could hardly have spent as much time in the city as he had without hearing them. His silence on the subject is not easily explained, the more so since his awareness of the practice is suggested elsewhere in the *Institution*. At the end of Chapter Four he discusses the manner in which the Lord's Supper ought to be administered. After the minister has excommunicated all who are unworthy of the sacrament, he is to pray that the congregation receive the bread and wine "with faith and thankfulness of heart," and that by God's "mercy" they be made "worthy of such a feast." [39] At this point, writes Calvin,

either psalms should be sung [*canerentur psalmi*], or something be read, and in becoming order the believers should partake of the most holy banquet, the ministers breaking the bread and giving the cup. When the Supper is finished, there should be an exhortation to sincere faith and confession of faith, to love and behavior worthy

of Christians. At the last, thanks should be given, and praises sung to God [*laudes Deo canerentur*].[40]

From the first reference to music it is clear that Calvin attaches no particular importance to its use, although he does specify that if the congregation sings, they are to sing psalms. Otherwise something should be read. It is just as clear, however, that he desires the celebration of the Lord's Supper to conclude with "praises sung to God," and in the *Institution* of 1536 this is the only unequivocal instruction for the use of song in public worship.[41]

IV. THE *ARTICLES* OF 1537

The change in his attitude as disclosed in the *Articles* of 1537 is thus remarkable. Song has been accorded now a necessary role in public worship. From a position essentially indifferent to its value Calvin has moved to one of very nearly unqualified acceptance. Moreover it is the psalms which are to be sung, and later in the *Articles* he indicates more explicitly why this should be so.

[35] *Institution*, p. 101; *OC* I, p. 89; *OS* 1, p. 104.

[36] For copious quotations from these songs, see Hasper, *Calvijns beginsel*, pp. 444–455; cf. *supra*, n. 23.

[37] *Institution*, p. 101; *OC* I, p. 89; *OS* 1, p. 104.

[38] Charles Garside, Jr., *Zwingli and the Arts* (New Haven/London, Yale University Press, 1966), p. 63; hereafter cited as Garside, *Zwingli*. Christoph Johannes Riggenbach, *Der Kirchengesang in Basel seit der Reformation. Mit neuen Aufschlüssen über die Anfänge des französischen Psalmengesangs, etc.* (Basel, 1870) was unavailable to me.

[39] *Institution*, p. 167; *OC* I: p. 140; *OS* 1: p. 161.

[40] *Ibid. Cf. Institution*, p. 153 [*OC* I, p. 129; *OS* 1, p. 149] where, speaking of the celebration of the Lord's Supper, Calvin argues that "it was ordained to be frequently used among all Christians in order that they might frequently return in memory to Christ's Passion, by such remembrance to sustain and strengthen their faith, and urge themselves to sing thanksgiving [*laudis canendam*], and to proclaim his goodness. . . ." It is significant that in both passages Calvin is thinking in terms of the practice of the apostolic church.

[41] The other references to music in the 1536 *Institution* are as follows: (1) Discussing ecclesiastical orders, Calvin cites Isidore's distinction between psalmists and readers: "He puts the psalmists in charge of the singing; . . ." [*Institution*, p. 220; *OC* I: p. 180; *OS* 1: p. 206]. Shortly thereafter he ridicules the over-subtle refinements of such orders: "For who most often lights the candles, pours wine and water into the cruet, but a boy or some wretched layman who gains his livelihood thereby? Do not the same men sing? Do not the same men shut and open the church doors?" [*Institution*, p. 223; *OC* I: p. 182; *OS* 1: pp. 208–209]. And finally he condemns the orders as "of no use or benefit in the church"; the latter, indeed, is "full of anathema . . . since it relegates to boys, the chanting [*cantiones*], which ought to have been heard only from consecrated lips." [*Institution*, p. 223; *OC* I: p. 183; *OS* 1: p. 209]. (2) With respect to the "lawful use of God's gifts," Calvin asserts that "we have never been forbidden to laugh, or to be filled, or to join new possessions to old and even ancestral ones, or to delight in musical harmony [*concentu musico*], or to drink wine." [*Institution*, p. 247; *OC* I: p. 200; *OS* 1: p. 228]. (3) On "the hours prescribed for public prayers, sermons, and baptisms," Calvin writes: "At sermons there are quiet and silence, appointed places, the singing together of hymns [*hymnorum concentus*], days set apart for the receiving of the Lord's Supper, the discipline of excommunications, and any others. The days themselves, the hours, the structure of the places of worship, what psalms are to be sung on what day, are matters of no importance." [*Institution*, p. 283; *OC* I: p. 227; *OS* 1: p. 257]. (4) There are, finally, two sentences where the passing reference to music is figurative: *Institution*, p. 228; *OC* I: p. 186; *OS* 1: p. 213, and *Institution*, p. 269; *OC* I: p. 217; *OS* 1: p. 246.

The other matter is the psalms which we wish to be sung in the church as we have it from the example of the ancient church and also the testimony of Saint Paul, who says that it is good to sing in the congregation with mouth and heart. We are not able to estimate the benefit and edification which will derive from this until after having experienced it. Certainly at present the prayers of the faithful are so cold that we should be greatly ashamed and confused. The psalms can stimulate us to raise our hearts to God and arouse us to an ardor in invoking as well as in exalting with praises the glory of His name. Moreover by this one will recognize of what advantage and consolation the pope and his creatures have deprived the church, for he has distorted the psalms, which should be true spiritual songs, into a murmuring among themselves without any understanding.[42]

Calvin acknowledges here for the first time his appreciation of the role which the psalms ideally can play in public worship. They possess, when sung, an extraordinary quality which can intensify communal prayer and praise of God by an appeal directed specifically to the worshipper's heart. The focus on the latter in this particular context derives from St. Paul; Calvin refers to, but does not actually cite, Colossians 3:16. Yet he is also in general reiterating the emphasis which he had laid on the proper disposition of the heart in the *Institution* of 1536. Gone, however, is his virtual silence on the question of joining song to public prayer. Its use instead is enthusiastically endorsed, for he is convinced now that the heart will respond appropriately to song if it is the *psalms* which are sung. And as if to emphasize this newly won conviction Calvin repeats, as he will elsewhere, the language of the sentence on psalmody in the opening paragraph of the *Articles*: singing the psalms has the power to arouse [*esmouyer*] and stimulate [*inciter*] our hearts, and in this fashion they can be raised [*esleuer*] to ardor [*ardeur*] in invoking and praising God.[43] The result will be an intensely emotional experience of worship which will differ not simply in degree, but in kind from the shamefully cold prayers now uttered in Geneva.

For the first time also Calvin rests his argument for a liturgical psalmody on an appeal to history. The *Articles* make clear that in addition to conformity to

the word of God, Calvin intended to reconstruct as far as was possible the worship as well as the discipline of the ancient church, and in that church, as Saint Paul testified, the psalms had been sung. Such singing, therefore, was fully as integral to Calvin's great vision of the whole life of the ancient church as was "that ancient, that is to say, apostolic, discipline of excommunication."[44] Psalmody was an *apostolic* practice, a fact of profound importance for Calvin,[45] underscored by his reference to the degeneration of contemporary liturgical music. After centuries of abuse by the papacy not even the priests understood what they were singing. Consequently the psalms were to be returned to the people, to whom they once belonged, to be sung by them in their own tongue, as once they had been, with understanding in the form of "true spiritual songs." Together with this explicit affirmation of psalmody, Calvin also renders implicitly a dismissive verdict: the singing of priests in Latin at the altar should be wholly eliminated from public worship, and this, in fact, would be the case in the Calvinist liturgy.[46]

In the space of a mere 146 words Calvin presented the council with a statement which constituted nothing less than the foundation for his theology of music. Much would be added to it later, but no one of the propositions which he laid down here would at any time be altered. Nor had he contented himself with an eloquent exposition of an ideal, for he had come as well to an exact decision as to how that ideal could be reduced to practice in Geneva.

The manner of beginning in this seemed to us well advised if some children who have previously practiced a modest church song sing in a loud and distinct voice, the people listening with complete attention and following with the heart what is sung with the mouth until little by little each one accustoms himself to singing communally.[47]

V. THE INFLUENCE OF BUCER

The whole passage is well known to students of Calvin. Hitherto unremarked, however, is the fact that it poses a considerable problem in Calvin's intellectual development: why did his attitude toward the role of music in worship change so markedly and so irrevocably from what he had written just a few years earlier in the *Institution*?

[42] *OC* **X**¹: p. 12; *OS* 1: p. 375: Laultre part est des pseaulmes, que nous desirons estre chantes en lesglise comme nous en auons lexemple en lesglise ancienne et mesme le tesmoignage de S. Paul, qui dict estre bon de chanter en la congregation de bouche et de cueur. Nous ne pouons concepuoyr laduancement et edification qui en procedera, sinon apres lauoyr experimente. Certes comme nous faysons, les oraysons des fidelles sont si froides, que cela nous doyt tourner a grand honte et confusion. Les pseaulmes nous pourront jnciter a esleuer noz cueurs a Dieu et nous esmouoyr a vng ardeur tant de linuocquer que de exalter par louanges la gloyre de son nom. Oultre par cela on pourra cognoestre de quel bien et de quelle consolation le pape et les siens ont priue lesglise, quant jl ont applicques les pseaulmes, qui doibuent estre vrays chants spirituel, a murmurer entre eux sans aulcune intelligence.

[43] On this special vocabulary, see Söhngen, *Calvin*, p. 57.

[44] Calvin to Bullinger, February 21, 1538. *OC* **X**²: No. 93: p. 154.

[45] Among Calvin scholars only F. W. Kampschulte has discerned the relationship. See his *Johann Calvin, seine Kirche und sein Staat in Genf*, two volumes in one (Geneva, Slatkine Reprints, 1972) 1: p. 288.

[46] Cf. Blankenburg, *Church Music*, pp. 516–517.

[47] *OC* **X**¹: p. 12; *OS* 1: p. 375: La maniere de y proceder nous a semble aduis bonne si aulcungs enfans, aux quelz on ayt auparauant recorde vng chant modeste et ecclesiastique, chantent a aulte voyx et distincte, le peuple escoutant en toute attention et suyuant de cueur ce qui est chante de bouche jusque a ce que petit a petit vng chascun se accoustemera a chanter communement.

Luther, of course, had always advocated and encouraged the full use of music in worship. His great contemporary, Huldrych Zwingli, however, did not share this point of view. In 1523, in the *Interpretation and Substantiation of the Conclusions,* he had considered the question of liturgical music under the rubric of prayer. Worship for him essentially *was* prayer, and ideally prayer ought to be silent. In defense of this position he had appealed especially to Matthew 6:6, and had concluded that ideally prayer should be an individual and private act rather than a corporate and public one. With respect to public worship, the necessity for which he did not deny, and which he wished to adhere as closely as possible to that of the early church, Zwingli prohibited singing, arguing in his *Apology on the Canon of the Mass* that "the words of Paul in Ephesians 5[19] and Colossians 3[16] concerning psaltery and singing in the heart give no help to those who protect their swan songs by them. For in the heart, he says, not with the voice [*in cordibus enim inquit, non vocibus*]. Therefore, the psalms and praises of God ought to be treated as if our minds sing to God." [48] The Apostle, as Zwingli interpreted him, had at no time been speaking literally of singing, and music of any sort in worship was therefore contrary both to Scripture and the practice of the early church. "As soon as it can be done," Zwingli urged, "this barbarous mumbling should be dispatched from the churches," [49] and two years later, in 1525, music was in fact eliminated from the liturgy of Zürich.

Almost simultaneously Martin Bucer had come to a conclusion on precisely this question of the use of music in public worship which was diametrically opposed to that of Zwingli. In the *Justification and Demonstration from Holy Scripture,*[50] published in 1524, he gave an account of the new liturgy of Strasbourg in considerable detail.

On Sundays when the congregation gathers together, the minister [*diener*] admonishes them to confess their sins and to pray for mercy, and makes confession to God for the whole congregation, prays for mercy, and proclaims to the faithful the absolution of sins. After that the whole congregation sings some short psalms or a song of praise. Then the minister says a brief prayer and reads to the congregation a selection from the writings of the Apostles and explains it as briefly as possible. Thereupon the congregation sings again: the ten commandments or something else. Afterwards the priest [*priester*] reads the Gospel and preaches the regular sermon. After that the congregation sings the articles of our faith [i.e., the Credo]. . . .[51]

A description of the preparation for the Lord's Supper and its administration follows. When all, including the minister, have communicated, then, says Bucer, "the congregation sings again: a song of praise." [52]

Moreover such congregational singing was not restricted to the celebration of the Lord's Supper.

At Vespers, since the material celebration should be used for the edification of the spirit, we sing one, two, or three psalms with a prophecy, that is, an explanation of something from a chapter from Holy Scripture. So also daily before and after the sermon a psalm is sung by the whole congregation.[53]

This extraordinary, perhaps even unprecedented, recourse to singing by the congregation was then defended by Bucer in the final chapter in which, discussing song and prayer, he emphatically denied that prayer should be silent for

in this we know that we are following the teaching of the Spirit of God, I Cor. 14 [1–40] and many other places. In Colossians 3[16] Paul also writes: Let the Word of God dwell in you richly in all wisdom, teach and admonish one another with psalms and songs of praise and spiritual songs in the mercy [of God], and sing to the Lord in your hearts. Similarly he wrote also to the Ephesians 5[19]. With all our might we are to love God. Why, then, should we not also sing to Him as all the saints of the Old and New Testament have done, provided that such song take place in the heart and not with the mouth only;

---

[48] Garside, *Zwingli,* p. 53; see pp. 27–75 for a detailed analysis of Zwingli's understanding of prayer and the reasons for his rejection of music from public worship.

[49] *Ibid.*

[50] Grund und ursach auss gotlicher schrifft der neüwerungen an dem nachtmal des herren, so man die Mess nennet, Tauff, Feyrtagen, bildern und gesang in der gemein Christi, wann die zůsamenkompt, durch und auff das wort gottes zů Strassburg fürgenomen, *Martin Bucers Deutsche Schriften,* 1, *Frühschriften 1520–1524,* herausgegeben von Robert Stupperich (Gütersloh, Gütersloher Verlagshaus Gerd Mohn, 1960), pp. 185–278; hereafter cited as *BDS.* For a translation with brief commentary, see Ottomar Frederick Cypris, *Basic Principles: Translation and Commentary of Martin Bucer's Grund und Ursach, 1524* (University Microfilms, Ann Arbor, Michigan, No. 71–26,379).

[51] *BDS* 1: p. 246: So am Sonnetag die gemein zůsamenkompt, ermant sye der diener zur bekantnüss der sünden und umb gnad zů bitten und beichtet gott anstat gantzer gemein, bit um gnad und verkündt den glaubigen abloss der sünden, auff das singt die gantz gemein etlich kurtz psalmen oder lobgesang. Dem nach thut der diener ein kurtz gebett und liset der gemein etwas von Apostel schrifften und verclert dasselbig auffs kürtzest. Daruff singt die gemein wider die zehen gebott oder etwas anders, alsdann so verkündt der priester das Evangelion und thut die recht predig, auff die singt die gemein die artickel unsers glaubens. . . .

[52] *BDS* 1: p. 247: Also bald singet die gemein wider ein lobgesang. . . .

[53] *BDS* 1: p. 275: Desgleichen zů vesperzeyt, seytenmal die leyplich feyr zů besserung des geists braucht werden sol, singet man aber ein psalmen, zwen oder drey mit einer propheti, das ist verklerung etwan eins capitels auss gotlicher schrifft, also auch taglich vor und nach der predig würt von gantzer gemein ein psalm gesungen.

but rather that it arise and come forth from the heart. This is what the Apostle means when he says: *and sing to the Lord in your hearts*, for his meaning is not that we sing without voice, for how could the others be admonished and edified, or how could we discuss with each other what he writes to the Ephesians.[54]

His emphasis on the importance of the heart is as unequivocal as that of Calvin; indeed, he had flatly asserted earlier that "it is a disgrace to God not to pray or sing with the heart." [55] But for Bucer there could be no disputing the fact that Paul intended singing to play an integral role in public worship.

Nor was his argument exclusively Scriptural. It was historical as well, for he continued by saying, surely in reply to Zwingli, that

those who decry the use of song in the congregation of God know little either about the content of Scripture or about the practice of the first and apostolic churches and congregations, which always praised God with song.[56]

Bucer had concluded that for this singing "the psalms are especially useful." [57] Again he turned to Scriptural and historical evidence, drawing now also on classical sources, for the practice of psalmody in the early church was recorded not only "in the writing of Paul and our histories, but also in pagan writings such as the witness of Pliny the Younger." [58] No warrant was more telling, however, than the single, central fact that "Christ Himself concluded His Last Supper and final sermon with a song of praise, Mat. 26[30]." [59]

The legitimacy of joining song to prayer thus irreproachably assured by Scripture, Bucer made clear that Scripture also provided the norm and content for

what was sung as well as said, for "in the congregation of God," he wrote, "we do not use songs or prayers which are not drawn from Scripture." [60] And finally these songs and prayers were in the vernacular so that the people could understand them and profit from their understanding.

Since what is done in the congregation of God should be beneficial to everyone in common, we neither pray nor sing anything except in common German speech, so that the laymen may in common say Amen, as the Holy Spirit teaches, 1. Corinth. 14[16].[61]

In 1530 the argument was compactly reiterated for the *Tetrapolitan Confession* in which Bucer seemed especially concerned to stress the idea of a return to the forms of apostolic worship. Scripture and the Fathers continued to be the norm for evaluation of the liturgy, and various aspects of contemporary ecclesiastical music, when measured against them, had been rejected because "their song has greatly deviated from the first usage of the holy fathers, as no one can deny." [62] The psalmody of the early church was Bucer's prime case in point. "From the writings of the fathers and the histories it is sufficiently well known that the early Christians in such Christian church services sang a very few psalms with the greatest devotion. . . ." [63] Furthermore the people understood what they were singing. Now, to the contrary, a situation prevails which is exactly the opposite: "a great many psalms are sung, but without comprehension and devotion." [64] Therefore the preachers in Strasbourg have eliminated from public worship everything which is not "in accordance with the word of God, as is their duty." [65] Significantly, however, Bucer concludes by insisting that such elimination is not to be interpreted negatively, but rather as a positive attempt to restore to the church the worship of the "ancient holy fathers." [66]

---

[54] *BDS* 1: pp. 275–276: Und in dem wissen wir, das wir der lere des geists gottes, 1. Cor. 14 [1–40] und anderswo mer nachfolgen. Zun Colossern 3 [16] schreibt auch Paulus: *Lasst das wort gottes in eüch wonen reyhlich in aller weyssheit, leret und vermanet eüch selbs mit psalmen und lobgesengen und geistlichen liedern in der gnad und singet dem herren in ewern hertzen*. Dergleichen hat er auch ad Eph. 5 [19]. Von allen krefften sollen wir je gott lieben, warumb solten wir im dann nit auch singen, wie alle heyligen des alten und newen testaments thon haben, allein das solich gesang im hertzen gescheh nit allein mit dem mund, sonder das es auss dem hertzen quelle und herkome. Das der Apostel damit meinet, da er spricht: *und singet dem herrn in ewern hertzen*, dann sein meinung nit ist, on stym zu singen, wie künten sust die andern ermanet und bessert werden oder wir mit einander reden, das er zun Ephesiern schreibt?

[55] *BDS* 1: p. 275: . . . ein schmach gottes ist, nit mit hertzen betten oder singen. . . .

[56] *BDS* 1: p. 276: Deshalb wissen die, so das gesang in der gemein gottes verwerffen, wenig weder umb der schrifft inhalt noch den brauch der ersten und Apostolischen kirchen und gemeinden, die alweg got auch mit gesang gelobet haben.

[57] *Ibid*: Dazu dan die psalmen sonderlich gebrauchet seind. . . .

[58] *Ibid*: . . . Des wir nit allein in schrifften Pauli und unsern hystorien sonder auch der heyden schrifft als namlich Plinii Secundi zeügnuss lesen.

[59] *Ibid*: So hat auch Christus selb sein nachtmal und letste predig mit eim lobgesang beschlossen, Mat. 26 [30].

[60] *BDS* 1: p. 275: . . . so gebrauchen wir uns in der gemein gots keins gesangs noch gepets, das nit auss götlicher schrifft gezogen sey. . . .

[61] *Ibid*: . . . dieweyl, was in der gemein gottes gehandelt würt, jederman in gemein besserlich sein soll, betten noch singen wir nichs, dann in gemeiner teütscher sprach, das der ley gemeincklich moge amen sprechen, wie das der geist gottes lernet, 1. Corinth. 14 [16].

[62] *BDS* 3: p. 147: Wellches gesang dann gar groblich von dem ersten prauch der haylligen vätter abkomen ist, wie das nyemanndt laugnen mag.

[63] *Ibid*: Dann aus der Vätter schryfft vnnd hystorien genuegsam bewust, das die allten in sollcher cristlicher kürchen Ybung ettlich wenig Psallmen mit höchster andacht gesungen haben. . . .

[64] *Ibid*: Nun singet man wol vil psallmen, aber on verstanndt vnnd andacht. . . .

[65] *BDS* 3: p. 149: Sollichs haben vnnsere Prediger an gewonlicher kürchen Yebung aus göttlichem wortt, wie sy schuldig sein, gestraffet.

[66] *BDS* 3: pp. 149–151: Es were inen aber nichtzit liebers, dann das sye solliche kürchenvbung vff die besserlichst weyss,

Zürich and Strasbourg were among the first cities of consequence to declare themselves reformed by officially abolishing the Mass, the former in 1525, the latter in 1529. Internal developments within both were observed, discussed, and widely reported, and their novel "evangelical" liturgies, the one without, the other with, music can have been no exception. Zwingli had been killed in battles in 1531, but was still widely read, and Bucer was steadily acquiring an international reputation. Calvin, to be sure, knew no German.[67] He could therefore have read neither the *Interpretation and Substantiation of the Conclusions* nor the *Justification and Demonstration from Holy Scripture,* but over the years their substance could easily have been made known to him. Moreover, the liturgical matter of the former was available in the Latin of Zwingli's *Apology on the Canon of the Mass*, while a summary of the latter was to be found in the Latin of the *Tetrapolitan Confession*. Detailed information about the prominent role of music in the Strasbourg liturgy could also have been conveyed to him personally by Gérard Roussel, who had witnessed it and described it with enthusiasm in two long letters written to friends at Meaux as early as December of 1525. Roussel, in fact, had been particularly impressed by the use of vernacular congregational psalmody in which "the singing of women together with the men was so wonderful that it was a delight to hear."[68] It is difficult, therefore, if not very nearly impossible, to believe that Calvin was not aware of the opposing conclusions on liturgical music of these prominent reformers when he was writing the first *Institution*.

In it the passages on music and prayer in the third chapter reveal an inclination, at the least, to Zwingli's position. As a matter of fact they form the climax to Calvin's exposition of Matthew 6:6, which was one of Zwingli's principal prooftexts for a liturgy without music. The content of the passages on psalmody in the *Articles* of 1537, on the other hand, is unmistakably Bucerian. In at least five recurrent emphases, all of which would have attracted Calvin immediately, the impact of his thinking may be observed. First of all, Bucer had insisted repeatedly that prayer, spoken or sung, must originate in the heart. Second, he had cast his liturgy wholly in the vernacular. Third, he was convinced that what was said and sung in it was derived from Scripture. Fourth, he had rested the use of song in worship securely on the evidence of Scripture and the usage of the early church. Fifth, all his liturgical efforts had been directed toward a restoration of the worship of that early church, and for Calvin, the life-long student of Christian antiquity, Bucer's appeal to history must have been in this regard decisive.[69] Why, then, did not Calvin initially adopt an expressly affirmative attitude toward the role of music in worship? How may we account for his reserve respecting the liturgical function of music in the *Institution* of 1536, especially when it is contrasted with the enthusiasm expressed so soon thereafter in the *Articles* of 1537? Given the evidence available there is no certain solution to the problem, but the following sequence in Calvin's inner development is ventured.

While in Basel he must have heard the congregational singing of psalms in the vernacular, but at the time all his attention was focused on completing the *Institution,* and, as the book clearly demonstrates, his concerns then were not liturgical. Psalmody does not go unmentioned, however, and the possibility that he intended to return to the relationship of music and worship and enlarge upon it at a later date cannot be overruled. Indeed, in the *Institution* of 1536 Calvin actually leaves small open spaces, *alinea* so-called, which correspond at least in part to points where later materials were inserted.[70]

---

so von hailligen allten Vättern gehallten, hetten widerpringen mögen, dann sy nichts weniger gewillt seind, Dann sollichs genntzlich abzustellen. *Cf.* the relevant portions of the *Apologie der Confessio Tetrapolitana, BDS* 3: pp. 292–299. See also Hughes Oliphant Old, *The Patristic Roots of Reformed Worship* (Zürich, Juris Druck Zürich, 1975), *passim,* but especially pp. 119–130; *cf.* pp. 39–42, and 80–87.

[67] Jacques Pannier, *Recherches sur la formation intellectuelle de Calvin* (Paris, Librairie Alcan, 1931), p. 22.

[68] Herminjard, I, No. 167: pp. 406–407: octava vero hora, aut eocirca contio fit in majori templo, adjunctis cantionibus in communem linguam ex hebraico psalterio transfusis, ubi mire assonant mulieres viris, ut jucundum sit audire; *ibid.,* No. 168, pp. 408–415. For a similarly enthusiastic reaction to the singing of men and women together, see *infra,* at n. 93. The description of the liturgy in No. 168 at pp. 412–413 is translated in Old, *op. cit.,* p. 71; *cf.* Bucer's own description (*BDS* 1: pp. 246–247), and *supra,* n. 51.

[69] I had become convinced of Bucer's influence on the development of Calvin's thinking about music before my reading of S. J. Lenselink, *De Nederlandse Psalmbereijmingen van de Souterliedekens tot Datheen, met hun voorgangers in Duitsland en Frankrijk* (Assen, Van Gorcum and Comp. N.V., 1959); hereafter cited as Lenselink, *De Nederlandse Psalmbereijmingen.* In the chapter on "Calvijns Principes" (pp. 158–169), he argues persuasively for Bucer's influence, but with an emphasis with which I cannot entirely agree. Calvin, he maintains, unlike Luther, with respect to church song created nothing new; he found it ready-made in 1539, "theory," texts, and melodies: "Wat de Franse reformator dan ook deed en schreef, was door en door, 'Straatsburg's'" (p. 158). Lenselink, to be sure, suggests that on Calvin's first visit to Strasbourg "at the end of 1534 and the beginning of 1535" (p. 158) he may have become acquainted with Bucer's ideas as expressed in the *Grund und Ursach,* but when he comes to demonstrate their influence his evidence is drawn from Calvin's *Epistre au Lecteur* which prefaces the Genevan Church Order of 1542 and the addition to it of 1543. Three of the most important Bucerian ideas which Lenselink adduces, however, (1) the identification of song with prayer, (2) the fact that both must come from the heart, and (3) the reliance on the authority of church history, are to be found in Calvin prior to 1542 or 1539; they appear unmistakably in the *Articles* of 1537. Lenselink is correct, I believe, in arguing for Bucer's influence, but Calvin had absorbed his ideas and expressed some of them in public even earlier.

[70] I owe this information to Professor Ford Lewis Battles.

In the early autumn of 1536, on the other hand, he had assumed pastoral responsibilities for the first time, and in this regard his situation could scarcely have been more changed. He was committed, albeit reluctantly, to the reform of the Genevan church in all its aspects, including its worship, and Farel's liturgy, which he encountered now, and of which, by virtue of his circumstances, he had to be fully conscious, was one without music.[71] There can be little doubt that it is precisely to this absence of music that Calvin referred when describing Genevan prayers as "cold." Confronted by a situation which he judged and condemned as "shameful," he must have recalled the "edification" to which congregational singing might lead as he knew it from the reports of Roussel and other French Evangelicals, his own experience in Basel, and Bucer's spirited insistence on the need for psalmody in public worship. A process of intense recollection and reevaluation undertaken within the new and exigent pastoral context of Geneva led him then in the closing months of 1536 to a fundamental reconsideration of worship music when preparing the *Articles*.

The psalmody Calvin proposed was not implemented, however. A variety of conditions, social, political, and theological, made his position in Geneva increasingly untenable, and during Easter Week of 1538 the situation came to a head in an open, indeed tumultuous, crisis. Bern, seeking uniformity in wor-

ship, had requested in March that Geneva subscribe to certain liturgical practices. The council agreed, but Calvin and Farel refused absolutely to comply, and as a result were banished summarily from the city on April 23. The two went at once to Bern to explain their conduct, and from there proceeded to the synod assembled at Zürich from April 29 to May 4. To it Calvin submitted a memorandum in fourteen articles in which he and Farel conceded the Bernese ceremonies while at the same time outlining their proposals for ecclesiastical reform in Geneva. Among these *Article XIII* required the singing of psalms in public worship.[72] Calvin's insistence on the practice, in spite of, and in the midst of, such controversy, reveals in striking fashion the depth of the commitment he had now made to congregational psalmody. The synod approved the proposals unanimously, but Geneva stood firm in its repudiation of Calvin's ministry, and roughly five months later he had settled in Strasbourg.

VI. CALVIN'S PASTORATE IN STRASBOURG

There Calvin immediately encountered that vernacular congregational psalmody which had been practiced in accordance with Bucer's ideas ever since 1524. At some time during the first two weeks in October, 1538, he wrote Farel informing him that for the celebration of the Lord's Supper he was using the Strasbourg liturgy,[73] and the assumption that this included the singing of psalms in the vernacular is confirmed by Johannes Zwick in a letter to Bullinger dated November 9.[74] But the intensity of Calvin's reaction to such psalmody is best gauged by the fact that on December 29, less than four months after his arrival in the city, he indicated to Farel that he was preparing a French psalter for his own congregation. He would, he said, publish the "psalms" shortly; he was even composing poetic versions of Psalms 46 and 25 himself.[75] In 1539[76] the psalter appeared bearing

---

An anonymous reader of the manuscript for the Society has also pointed out that the 1536 *Institutio* was intended as a manual of instruction for French Protestants who were meeting secretly for Bible study and prayer. Singing would have invited discovery and detention. Under such circumstances, therefore, any lengthy consideration of psalmody would have been inappropriate to the first edition.

[71] See Hugh Y. Reyburn, *John Calvin. His Life, Letters, and Work* (London, Hodder and Stoughton, 1914), p. 63, and Hasper, *Calvijns beginsel*, p. 431. Farel's approbation of the *Articles* of 1537 clearly demonstrates that he was not opposed to the introduction of singing into public worship, but I find no evidence for Hasper's assertion (p. 444) that for sometime earlier he had been an advocate of the practice. Doumergue, *Calvin* 2: p. 506, n. 3 notes that some *Noelz nouveaulx* and seven other songs were bound with Farel's *La manière et fasson* (see below), but this by no means indicates that they were intended for liturgical use. There is no reference to music in *La manière et fasson quon tient es lieux que Dieu de sa grâce a visités* (Première liturgie des Églises réformées de France de l'an 1533. Publiée d'après l'original à l'occasion du troisième jubilé séculaire de la constitution de ces églises l'an 1559, par Jean-Guillaume Baum. Strasbourg/Paris, 1859), nor in the *Sommaire et Briefve Declaration*; see *Le Sommaire de Guillaume Farel* (Reimprime d'après l'édition de l'an 1534 et précédé d'une introduction par J.-G. Baum, Genève, Jules-Guillaume Fick, 1867), and *Sommaire et Briefve Declaration* (Fac-similé de l'édition originale, publié sous le patronage de la Société des textes français modernes par Arthur Piaget, Paris, Librairie E. Droz, 1935). *Cf.* Henri Vuilleumier, *Histoire de l'église réformée du Pays de Vaud sous le régime bernois* (Lausanne, Éditions La Concorde, 1927) 1: p. 329, and Doumergue, *Calvin,* 2: p. 506, especially n. 3.

[72] *OC* **X**²*,* No. 111: p. 192; Herminjard, **V**, No. 708, p. 6: XIII. Alterum, ut ad publicas orationes Psalmorum cantio adhibeatur. [Correct "cantus" to "cantio" in Pidoux, *Documents,* p. 2]. Bern, following Zwingli's decision in Zürich, had abolished worship music (Blankenburg, *Church Music,* pp. 510–511). Herminjard, *ibid.,* n. 16, suggests that Calvin's insistence on psalmody may have influenced Bernese practice, for the Manual of Bern under the date Wednesday, June 21, 1538, reads as follows: "Write a letter to the judges of the Consistory informing them that *Messieurs* desire that the young learn to sing *the Psalms,* and that the director of the School and his chief of instruction teach the music of the said psalms."

[73] Calvin to Farel, October, 1538, *OC* **X**²*,* No. 149: p. 279; Herminjard, **V**, No. 751, p. 145.

[74] Zwick to Bullinger, November 9, 1538. *OC* **X**²*,* No 151: p. 288: Gallis Argentorati ecclesia data est in qua a Calvino quater in septimana conciones audiunt, sed et coenam agunt et psalmos sua lingua canunt. *Cf.* Herminjard, **V**, No. 751: p. 145, n. 19; also Pidoux, *Documents,* p. 2.

[75] Calvin to Farel, December 29, 1538. *OC* **X**²*,* No. 200: p. 438; Herminjard, **V**, No. 762a: pp. 452–453: Psalmos ideo

the title *Aulcuns pseaulmes et cantiques mys en chant*.[77] Calvin had edited it; of that there is no doubt.[78] It contained nineteen psalms in French translation, all but one of which (No. 113) were rhymed. Thirteen of these were by Clément Marot,[79] and Calvin was responsible for the remainder.[80] The versions of the

Song of Simeon, the Decalogue, and the Credo are his also,[81] so that this, his first psalter, unlike later versions, is peculiarly his book. Exceptionally fortunate in the availability of the psalms of Marot, he was equally fortunate in having at hand the music of Matthäus Greitter and Wolfgang Dachstein, for both were "composers of particular artistic worth."[82]

While working on the psalter, Calvin had been at the same time concluding a second edition of the *Institution*. Extensively revised and enlarged, it, too, was published in 1539. In it the chapter on prayer was expanded at several points, but of all the alterations and additions none was more significant for our purposes than the phrase which Calvin added to the discussion of the use of voice and song in prayer. In 1536 he had written: "Yet we do not here condemn speaking and singing provided they are associated with the heart's affection and serve it."[83] For the new edition, between "singing" and "provided" he inserted the words "but rather strongly commend them [*quin potius valde commendamus*]." He also deleted the phrase "and serve it [*eique serviant*]," doubtless to ameliorate somewhat his earlier insistence on the subservient role of music. The sentence now read: "Yet we do not here condemn speaking and singing but rather strongly commend them, provided they are associated with the heart's affection."[84] It is, of

---

miseramus, ut prius cantarentur apud vos, quam illuc pervenirent quo intelligis. Statuimus enim brevi publicare. Quia magis arridebat melodia Germanica, coactus sum experiri quid carmine valerem. Ita Psalmi duo, 46. et 25., prima sunt mea tyrocinia: alios postea attexui. For the year in which the letter was written I follow Herminjard, **V**: pp. 446–447, n. 1. *Cf.* Pidoux, *Documents*, p. 2, and Samuel Jan Lenselink, *Les Psaumes de Clément Marot*, p. 24, n. 1, who accepts 1538, but dates the letter 19 rather than 29 December.

[76] On the basis of evidence incorrectly read (see Herminjard, *op. cit., supra*, n. 75), Markus Jenny has argued for 1540. See "Untersuchungen zu den Aulcuns Pseaumes (sic) et Cantiques mys en chant à Strasbourg 1539," *Jahrbuch für Liturgik und Hymnologie 2. Jahrgang* 1956 (Kassel, Johannes Stauda-Verlag, 1957): pp. 109–110.

[77] The Bayerische Staatsbibliothek in Munich possesses the only copy known of this psalter, discovered by Orentin Douen and described, albeit inadequately in view of its importance, in his *Clément Marot et le psautier huguenot* (Paris, Imprimerie Nationale, 1878–1879), **I**: pp. 302–303. Not until 1919 was it published in a facsimile edition of 500 copies briefly introduced by D. Delétra: *Aulcuns pseaulmes et cantiques mys en chant a Strasburg 1539. Réimpression phototypographique précédée d'un avant-propos par D. Delétra*, Genève, A. Jullien, 1919. It is available in facsimile also in *Calvin's First Psalter [1539]*, edited with critical notes and modal harmonies to the melodies by Sir Richard Runciman Terry (London, Ernest Benn Limited, 1932), Part I, pp. 1–65, and in H. Hasper, *Calvijns beginsel*, pp. 456–471. Terry's suggestion (p. v) that initially Calvin may not have prepared the Strasbourg Psalter for liturgical use is untenable. For bibliographical comment, see Pidoux, *Documents*, p. 3; *cf.* also his strictures against the "critical notes and modal harmonies" of Terry's edition in the *Jahrbuch für Liturgik und Hymnologie, op. cit.*, p. 109. The postscript of a letter (dated June 28, 1539) from Pierre Toussain, the pastor at Montbéliard, to Calvin requesting the "psalmos gallicos" indicates that the psalter had by then been published; see *OC* **X²**, No. 176: p. 357, and Herminjard, **V**, No. 799, p. 345. On October 27, 1539 Calvin notified Farel that 100 copies had been sent to Geneva; see *OC* **X²**, No. 194: p. 426, and Herminjard, **VI**, No. 832: p. 118. On the first Strasbourg liturgy, see Dora Scheuner, "Calvins Genfer Liturgie und seine Strassburger Liturgie textgeschichtlich dargestellt," *Das Wort sie sollen lassen stahn, Festschrift für D. Albert Schädelin* (Bern, Verlag Herbert Lang und Cie, 1950), pp. 79–85, and *idem., OS* 2: pp. 1–5. Blankenburg, *Calvin*, col. 664, rightly observes about her "lost" edition that "nur vermutungsweise etwas gesagt werden kann." *Cf.* also Robert Will, "La première liturgie de Calvin," *Revue d'histoire et de philosophie religieuses* 18, Nos. 5–6 (November-December, 1938): pp. 523–529. Alfred Erichson, *Die calvinische und die altstrassburgische Gottesdienstordnung. Ein Beitrag zur Geschichte der Liturgie in der Evangelischen Kirche . . .* (Strassburg, J. H. E. Heitz, 1894) was unavailable to me.

[78] Blankenburg, *Church Music*, p. 517.

[79] Nos. 1, 2, 3, 15, 19, 32, 51 (50), 103, 114 (113), 115, 130 (129), 137, and 143 (142). The problem of how Calvin obtained these texts remains unsolved; see especially Samuel Jan Lenselink, *Les Psaumes de Clément Marot*, p. 23.

[80] Nos. 25, 36, 46, 91 (90), 113, and 138. For the com-

plete texts of all of Calvin's psalms, the Song of Simeon, the Ten Commandments, and the *cantique* "Salutation a Iesus Christ," see *OC* **VI**: pp. 211–224. An English translation of the last is to be found in Philip Schaff, *Christ in Song* (New York, 1869), pp. 678–680. The texts of the six psalms in the 1539 psalter are reproduced with facing English translation by Ford Lewis Battles, *The Piety of John Calvin. An Anthology Illustrative of the Spirituality of the Reformer of Geneva* (Pittsburgh, Pittsburgh Theological Seminary, 1969), pp. 169–188. See also Adolph Zahn, "Calvin als Dichter," *Zeitschrift für kirchliche Wissenschaft und kirchliches Leben* 10 (1889): pp. 315–319.

[81] Pidoux, *Documents*, p. 3, n. 7, observes that the attribution to Calvin of Psalms 25 and 46 cannot be questioned. Calvin's authorship of the others, however, although uncontested, is less demonstrably certain, especially with respect to Psalm 113 and the Credo, and perhaps the Song of Simeon. *Cf.* the caution expressed in *John Calvin: Six Metrical Psalms. An English Translation by Ford Lewis Battles Set to the Original Melodies of the Strassburg Psalter of 1539 As Harmonized by Sir Richard R. Terry [1932]* (Pittsburgh, The Pittsburgh Theological Seminary, 1969), p. 1.

[82] Blankenburg, *Church Music*, p. 519. On Greitter (Greiter), see *Die Musik in Geschichte und Gegenwart*, 5 (1956): cols. 799–802; on Dachstein, *ibid.*, 15 (1973): col. 1683.

[83] *Institution*, p. 100; *OC* **I**: p. 88; *OS* 1: p. 103: Neque tamen vocem aut cantum hic damnamus, modo animi effectum sequantur eique serviant.

[84] *Calvin: Institutes of the Christian Religion*, edited by John T. McNeill and translated by Ford Lewis Battles, *The Library of Christian Classics* (Philadelphia, The Westminister Press, 1960) 21: p. 894; hereafter cited as *Institutes*. *Cf. OC* **II**: p. 658; *OS* 4: p. 341: Neque tamen vocem aut cantum hic damnamus, quin potius valde commendamus, modo animi affectum comitentur.

course, impossible to ascertain when Calvin decided to make the addition, but the assumption may not unreasonably be made that it was at Strasbourg while he was completing the final revision. He had recommended psalmody initially to the council in Geneva in 1537. Somewhat over a year later, in the spring of 1538, he had urged it again before the larger audience of the synod of Zürich. Now in 1539, his "strong commendation" of the practice, written perhaps even as he was editing the psalter, was acknowledged for the first time to the Latin-reading public of Europe, and therein lies its special significance. The approbation was permanent as well, for it would stand in all future editions of the *Institution*.

VII. THE *ECCLESIASTICAL ORDINANCES*

On September 13, 1541, Calvin reentered Geneva. That same day he met with the council, and having assured them that thereafter he would always be the servant of Geneva, he asked that "order be established in the church, and that it be put in writing." [85] The request was immediately honored, and somewhat over two months later, on November 20, the three councils approved the *Ecclesiastical Ordinances*.

The ecclesiastical and civil frame of reference for the document remained fundamentally that of the *Articles*. During Calvin's retreat in Strasbourg the church in Geneva had disintegrated; political and social conditions were scarcely better, so that the imperative for "good order" was demonstrably as urgent late in 1541 as it had been early in 1537. Nor had Calvin in the intervening years deviated in the slightest from his insistence that the order for the church should conform as nearly as possible to Scripture and the practice of the ancient church. Between the two documents, then, there is a continuity both of context and purpose.

Music, however, in contrast to the *Articles*, is barely mentioned in the *Ordinances*, in all likelihood because Calvin had resolved to take up the subject separately. In the entire document, as a matter of fact, there are only two sentences devoted to the subject, and even their position in the text is peculiar, indeed inexplicable, for they stand, not by themselves under a separate rubric, but randomly within the paragraph on marriage and matrimonial problems.

It will be good to introduce ecclesiastical songs, the better to incite the people to pray to and praise God.
For a beginning the little children are to be taught; then with time all the church will be able to follow.[86]

The content of the two sentences is almost identical with that of the concluding paragraph on music in the

Articles. Calvin was still persuaded that the responsibility for introducing congregational singing into public worship lay first with the children. The city schools, however, such as they were, unlike those of Basel, for instance, as yet afforded no such education. The proposal that "little children are to be taught" is thus one of far-reaching significance, for it marks the effective beginning of musical education in sixteenth-century Geneva.[86a]

VIII. THE *EPISTLE TO THE READER*: 1542

The *Ordinances* completed, during the following year and the first six months of 1543 Calvin was to be uniquely preoccupied with the question of the liturgical function of music. For the remainder of his life he would, to be sure, discuss it many times in his commentaries and sermons, occasionally at some length, but never again would he write so much about it in so short a time. He concluded the *Epistle to the Reader* for his order of worship for Geneva (1542) with a brief statement (193 words) on prayer and song. He also enlarged the chapter on prayer in the revised *Institution* of 1543 with an account of singing in the early church together with further considerations on the nature of psalmody (289 words). And finally in 1543 he returned to the *Epistle to the Reader* which had prefaced *The Form of Prayers* and added to it, as earlier noted, his longest single statement on the subject (918 words). The passages were written separately, on three different occasions, but they may be understood properly only if they are read as a single, interrelated, progressively more comprehensive and more profound reflection on music and worship, and, at the last, on the very nature of music itself.

The importance of the relationship which he now perceived between public prayer and song, as well as the high priority which it had attained at that time in his mind, is immediately conveyed by the title of the order: *The Form of Prayers and Ecclesiastical Songs, with the manner of administering the sacraments and consecrating marriage according to the custom of the ancient Church.*[87] It was prefaced by an *Epistle to the Reader,* the superintending theme of which was Calvin's intense concern for the benefit and education of

---

[85] *OC* **XXI**: p. 282.

[86] *OC* **X**[1]: p. 26: Jl sera bon dintroduyre les chantz ecclesiastiques pour mieulx jnciter le peuple a pryer et louer dieu.

Pour le commencement on apprendra les petiz enfans, puys avec le temps toutte lesglise pourra suyvre.

[86a] See Ferdinand Buisson, *Sébastien Castellion, sa vie et son oeuvre 1515–1563* (Nieuwkoop, B. De Graaf, 1964) **1**: p. 149: "Une seule innovation importante s'était faite depuis le retour de Calvin [to Geneva in 1541], et elle donna sans doute au collège de Castellion une vie qui n'avait pas eue le collège de Saunier. C'est l'introduction du chant des psaumes." *Cf.* Pidoux, *Documents,* p. 11.

[87] *OC* **VI**: pp. 165–172; *OS* **2**: pp. 11–18: LA FORME DES PRIERES ET CHANTZ ECCLESIASTIQUES, auec la maniere d'administrer les Sacremens et consacrer le Mariage: selon la coustume de l'Eglise ancienne. The Württembergische Landesbibliothek in Stuttgart possesses the only copy known of this edition. It was published in facsimile (Edition Bärenreiter Kassel et Bâle, 1959), "avec une notice par Pierre Pidoux" (pp. 3–8).

the worshipper. For this the fundamental prerequisite was understanding, and this, in turn, meant the use of the vernacular in public worship. "If we wish truly," he writes,

to honor the holy ordinances of our Lord which we use in the Church, the most important thing is to know what they contain, what they mean, and to what purpose they tend, in order that their observance may be useful and salutary, and in consequence rightly regulated.[88]

These ordinances comprise three things, preaching, public prayers, and the administration of the sacraments. Preaching he does not discuss. Prayers he treats briefly, and the sacraments at somewhat greater length.

And then, towards the close, Calvin returns to the subject of public prayers, dividing them into "two kinds: the ones made with the word only, the others with song." [89] "And this," he maintained, "is not a thing invented a short time ago." [90] On first reading the sentence is a curious one. It must not be forgotten, however, that in the first *Institution* Calvin's reserve about the addition of song to prayer, private or public, had been unconcealed. In the whole book its use had been recommended only once and for a specific occasion: the conclusion of the celebration of the Lord's Supper. He had added the commendation of song to the edition of 1539 as well as deleting the phrase "and serve it," but otherwise had left the earlier text unaltered. The first French edition of 1541 was a translation from the Latin of 1539, adding at this point nothing new. The Strasbourg Psalter had appeared without a preface. What Calvin had written thus far affirming the necessity for the introduction of song

into worship had been in the form of memoranda, one directed only to the Genevan council, the other to the synod of Zürich. The conclusion to the *Epistle* of 1542 was his first statement on church music expressly written for the people of the city, and those elsewhere who would read it. It was necessary, therefore, to explain to this new and considerably larger audience, as it had been necessary in 1537 to explain to the Genevan council, why song and prayer should be joined together. Furthermore such vernacular congregational singing was a phenomenon associated intimately, if not inextricably, with the advancement of the Reformation, and as such was, in point of fact, of very recent origin. It was just as necessary, therefore, to make clear, as had Bucer so many times before him, that the psalmody which he was proposing was a matter not of wanton innovation but of pious restoration. To sing prayers publicly was to return, as the title of the order explicitly stated, to "the custom of the ancient Church [*selon la coustume de l'Eglise ancienne*]," a fact which Calvin emphasized in the next two sentences: "for from the first origin of the Church, this has been so, as appears from the histories. And even Saint Paul speaks not only ₔof praying by mouth, but also of singing." [91]

In its identical sequence of appeals to authority, first to that of the ancient church and then to that of St. Paul, the statement immediately recalls the *Articles* of 1537. "And in truth," Calvin continues, "we know from experience that song has great force and vigor to arouse and inflame the hearts of men to invoke and praise God with a more vehement and ardent zeal." [92] Here, too, in the cluster of words such as *esmouvoir, enflamber, vehement, ardent,* and *zele* the langage is exactly like that of the earlier document, but the similarity in fact serves to emphasize what is both different and altogether new in the *Epistle.* What had been uppermost in Calvin's mind when writing the *Articles* had been the text; it was the *psalms,* when sung, which could bring a peculiar emotional and spiritual intensity to public worship. Now he turns to a consideration of the *music,* a consideration which derives, as he is careful to record, *"par experience."* For an understanding of the development of his theology of music the autobiographical phrase is crucial.

With respect to Calvin's information about vernacular congregational psalmody, derived either from his reading or from reports from friends and acquaintances, there can be little, if indeed any, doubt. On the other hand, the extent of his *personal* knowledge

---

[88] *OC* **VI**: pp. 165–166; *OS* **2**: p. 13: Pourtant, si nous voulons bien honnorer les sainctes ordonnances de nostre Seigneur, desquelles nous usons en l'Eglise, le principal est de scavoir, qu'elles contiennent, qu'elles veullent dire, et à quelle fin elles tendent: afin que l'usage en soit utile et salutaire, et par consequent droictement reiglé. Conforming to Calvin's usage, the word Church will be capitalized in citations from the *Epistle.*

[89] *OC* **VI**: pp. 167–169; *OS* **2**: p. 15: Quant est des prieres publiques, il y en a deux especes. Les unes se font par simple parolle: les aultres avecque chant. The analysis of the 1542 text which follows, as well as that of the addition of 1543, supersedes that in Charles Garside, Jr., "Calvin's Preface to the Psalter: A Re-Appraisal," *The Musical Quarterly* **37**, No. 4 (October, 1951): pp. 566–577 at pp. 567–575. The comments on the preface by Fritz Büsser, "Calvin und die Kirchenmusik," *Musik und Gottesdienst* **3** (1949): pp. 97–106 at pp. 99–103 are expository rather than analytical or interpretive, and take no account of the development of Calvin's thought. Much the same may be said of the brief article by Dorothy Boyd, "Calvin's Preface to the French Metrical Psalms," *Evangelical Quarterly* **22** (October, 1950): pp. 249–254, which is also marred by impermissibly free translation. Yorke Bannard, "Calvin as Musical Reformer," *The Monthly Musical Record* **49**, No. 583 (July, 1919): pp. 151–152 simply gives three extracts from the *Epistle* with a cursory introduction.

[90] *OC* **VI**: pp. 169–170; *OS* **2**: p. 15: Et n'est pas chose inventee depuis peu de temps.

[91] *Ibid:* Car des la premiere origine de l'Eglise, cela a esté; comme il appert par les histoires. Et mesmes sainct Paul ne parle pas seulement de prier de bouche, mais aussi de chanter.

[92] *Ibid:* Et à la verité, nous congnoissons par experience, que le chant a grand force et vigueur d'esmouvoir et enflamber le coeur des hommes, pour invoquer et louer Dieu d'un zele plus vehement et ardent.

and awareness of the efficacy of the practice prior to his arrival in Strasbourg in 1538 may legitimately be questioned. There are no marked indications of it in the *Institution* of 1536. The *Articles* of 1537 emphatically endorse psalmody, but in these Calvin admitted to the fact that "we are not able to estimate the benefit and edification which will derive from this [psalmody] until after having experienced it [*sinon apres lauoyr experimente*]." In the context of the enthusiasm for singing the psalms which Calvin was enunciating so forcefully, the sentence is difficult to interpret, but if nothing else it points to an uncertainty in his mind as to how the citizens of Geneva would react to such a liturgical innovation. And this uncertainty in turn points to the possibility at least that he was as yet personally unsure of the emotional and spiritual dimensions which music could add to public worship. If such doubts in fact existed, his pastoral experience in Strasbourg had completely and permanently eliminated them.

Calvin had had his own congregation there, and from his own parishioners he had quickly learned at first hand the depth of their appreciation for the singing of the psalms in their own language. How much, in fact, it meant to them is revealed in a letter by a young man from Antwerp who had sought refuge in Strasbourg during Easter Week of 1545. Sometime thereafter he wrote to his cousins at Lille as follows:

On Sundays . . . we sing a psalm of David or some other prayer taken from the New Testament. The psalm or prayer is sung by everyone together, men as well as women with a beautiful unanimity, which is something beautiful to behold. For you must understand that each one has a music book in his hand; that is why they cannot lose touch with one another. Never did I think that it could be as pleasing and delightful as it is. For five or six days at first, as I looked upon this little company, exiled from countries everywhere for having upheld the honor of God and His Gospel, I would begin to weep, not at all from sadness, but from joy at hearing them sing so heartily, and, as they sang, giving thanks to the Lord that He had led them to a place where His name is honored and glorified. No one could believe the joy which one experiences when one is singing the praises and wonders of the Lord in the mother tongue as one sings them here.[93]

Perhaps no other contemporary source articulates so vividly one individual's reaction to vernacular congregational psalmody. The letter was written, to be sure, after Calvin had returned to Geneva, but the emotions described by the young Walloon can yet have been little different from those of members of Calvin's own French-speaking congregation. It was a response to song such as this that moved him so swiftly to prepare his first psalter. It may also have led him to insert the commendation of song into the revised *Institution* of 1539. It is certainly as a result of such a response that he speaks for the first time publicly "from experience" in the *Epistle to the Reader* of 1542. After his years, even his first months, in Strasbourg, Calvin could and would speak of the power of music with a knowledge and a certainty which he cannot be said definitively to have possessed before.

Given his full awareness of its enormous potentiality for intensifying the public praise of God, it is not surprising that Calvin insists by way of antithesis that "there must always be concern that the song be neither light nor frivolous, but have gravity [*pois*] and majesty [*maiesté*], as Saint Augustine says."[94] Although he does not explain further what he intends by the words *pois* and *maiesté*, it is abundantly clear that he has in mind some kind of ecclesiastical music the *unique* character of which is underscored in what follows: "And thus there is a great difference between the music which one makes to entertain men at table

---

[93] Les dimanches . . . on chante quelque psaulme de David ou une aultre oroison prinse du nouveau testament, laquelle psaulme ou oroison se chante touts ensemble, tant homme que femme avecq ung bel accord, laquelle chose est bel a veoir. Car il vous fault entendre que chascun a ung libvre de musicque en sa main, voila pourquoy il ne se peulvent desborder; je neuse jamais pensé qu'il eut este tant plaisant et delectable comme il est. Je fust bien cincq ou six jours au commenchement, quant je voioie ceste petite assemblée laquelle estant expulsée de touts pays pour avoir maintenu l'honneur de Dieu et son evangille, je commenchoie à pleurer, non point par trystesse mais de joie en les oians chanter de sy bon coeur, comme il chantent, rendant grace au Seigneur, quil luy a plut les amener en plache où son nom est honnouré et glorifié. Jamais creature ne sauroit croire la joie que on a quant on

chante les louenges et merveilles du Seigneur en la langue maternelle comme on chante ichy. Alfred Erichson, *L'Église française de Strasbourg au seizième siècle d'après des documents inédits* (Strasbourg, Librairie C. F. Schmidt, 1886), pp. 21–22; *cf.* the similar sentiments in the letter to Jean Du Bois, *ibid.*, p. 15.

[94] *OC* **VI**: pp. 169–170; *OS* 2: p. 15: Il y a tousiours à regarder, que le chant ne soit pas legier et volage: mais ait pois et maiesté, comme dit sainct Augustin. For the influence of Augustine on Calvin, see the fundamental study of Luchesius Smits, *Saint Augustin dans l'oeuvre de Jean Calvin*, two volumes (Assen, Van Gorcum and Comp. N.V., 1957–1958), *passim*; for the references to Augustine in the *Epistle*, ten in all, consult 2: pp. 67–68. The source in Augustine for the requirement that the song have gravity and majesty remains unidentified. Oliver Strunk, *Source Readings in Music History. From Classical Antiquity through the Romantic Era* (New York, W. W. Norton and Company, Inc., 1950), p. 346, proposed *Epistola LV*, xviii, 34. There, however, Augustine is speaking not about a musical style, but the manner [*sobrie*] in which the psalms are sung. Neither the words gravity and majesty nor their equivalents are to be found in the passage. The same objections must be made to *Confessions* **X**: p. 33 cited by Dora Scheuner, *OS* 2: p. 15, and Smits, *op. cit.* 2: p. 68. Lenselink, *De Nederlandse Psalmbereijmingen*, p. 159, observes that Calvin's insistence on gravity and majesty is the first idea with respect to music in the *Epistle* not to be found in Bucer. He adds that it is not therefore un-Bucerian, a statement which is indefensible, for Bucer never concerned himself with a search for a special kind of ecclesiastical music. It is at this point precisely that Calvin's originality asserts itself.

and in their homes, and the psalms which are sung in the Church in the presence of God and His angels. [95]

Luther had openly proclaimed his desire to use all available music, including the most obviously secular, for the worship of the church. The fact that he placed so few, if any, restrictions on the music to be employed led to the creation of the so-called contrafacta, that is to say popular songs, whose melodies were well and widely known, adopted to liturgical use by means of new texts. These

ranged from the 'Christian improvement' of single words (which may be considered contrafacta in the broadest sense of the term), through the new sacred interpretation of secular texts and the Protestant rewriting of Catholic texts . . . to the supplying of a completely new text for a melody without regard to the emotional content and subject of the original verse; finally, several different new texts could be written for one and the same melody, older melodies could be furnished with texts belonging to other tunes, and whole groups of poetic lied texts could be organized more or less mechanically around a single melody, in reliance upon its musical popularity. [96]

Such varieties of technique notwithstanding, what mattered most was the people's prior knowledge of the melody, sacred or secular, for by means of it they could be led "to the apprehension of [Protestant] truth through familiar sound." [97]

Calvin, to the contrary, now absolutely rejects such a deployment of existing musical resources. The two phrases "at table" and "in their homes" serve as focusing rubrics under which he understands *all* secular music, and this is music for entertainment. Over against it he sets music for worship. The musical character of one is light [*legier*] and frivolous [*volage*]; the musical character of the other must be grave and majestic. To one no words are necessarily attached; to the other the text of the psalms. The one, by implication, may be either instrumental or vocal or any combination of both; the other, also in this context by implication, is exclusively vocal. Above all, the one is designed for men, while the other is for God and His angels. The antithesis between the secular and the sacred could scarcely be more pointed, [98] and

it is surely significant that Calvin has placed the two sentences penultimately in the *Epistle*; to set purpose he has reserved his definition of the *Chantz ecclesiastiques* for a place of special prominence at the end. [99] That done, he concludes with the hope that his order of worship might be found "holy and pure, seeing that it is simply directed to the edification of which we have spoken." [100]

It would be difficult to overestimate the importance of Calvin's decision to exclude the use of any secular music from his liturgy. His intention, as bold as it was novel, to break as decisively as possible with both musical past and musical present sets his theology of music fundamentally and permanently apart from that of Luther. By the same token his intention to create an ecclesiastical music which was, insofar as such was possible, wholly new, marks the beginning of what would form the distinctive character of Calvinist psalmody, namely what Blankenburg has designated "the sacred style." [101] By this he means that Calvin was not so much concerned with the musical setting of a particular text as he was with a style "*generally* fitting the sacred service," [102] and this, in fact, Calvin eventually would achieve in the melodies of the Genevan Psalter. When, therefore, in this, its first edition, immediately under the title of the order he put the opening line of Psalm 96, [103] "Sing to the Lord a new Song," his understanding of the injunction was more literal and consequently far more radical than would at first sight appear.

IX. THE *INSTITUTION* OF 1543

The justification of psalmody in the *Epistle* was brief; it was written in the vernacular, and published as an introduction to an order of worship specifically for Geneva. Brevity, language, and format must have weighed on Calvin's mind as he reviewed the exposition of prayer in the *Institution,* for in it there was nothing on the relationship of music and prayer comparable to what he had written in the *Epistle*. Merely to commend speaking and singing "strongly," with the qualification that they be "associated with the heart's affection," was now inadequate. Clearly more than this was required if Calvin's learned audience was to

---

[95] *OC* **VI**: pp. 169–170; *OS* 2: p. 15: . . . et ainsi il y ait grande différence entre la musicque qu'on faict pour resiouyr les hommes à table et en leur maison: et entre les psalmes, qui se chantent en l'Eglise, en la presence de Dieu et de ses anges.

[96] Friedrich Blume, *Protestant Church Music, A History* (New York, W. W. Norton and Company, Inc., 1974), p. 30.

[97] *Ibid.*

[98] Lenselink, *De Nederlandse Psalmbereijmingen,* p. 159, simply acknowledges that this differentiation is not to be found in Bucer. Its crucial significance is stressed, on the other hand, by Blankenburg, *Calvin,* cols. 660–661: "Somit unterscheidet Calvin nicht nur grundsätzlich zwischen gottesdienstlicher und aussergottesdienstlicher, sondern noch weitergehend zwischen geistlicher und weltlicher Musik. An diesem Punkte entfernt er sich am weitesten von Luthers Musikanschauung. Den Begriff der Kontrafaktur kennt er im Grunde nicht, da geistlich und weltlich für ihn zwei getrennte Sphären sind."

[99] *Cf.* Söhngen, *Calvin,* p. 46: "Calvin lehnte also die musikalische Einheit zwischen geistlichem und weltlichem Lied bewusst ab und forderte statt dessen einem EIGENEN KIRCHLICHEN, SAKRALEN STIL; *chant ecclésiastique* ist nicht nur wörtliche Übersetzung des römischen *cantus ecclesiasticus,* sondern hat auch den gleichen bedeutungsgeschichtlichen Sinn eines spezifischen, nur der Kirche und dem Gottesdienst zugehörigen Gesanges."

[100] *OC* **VI**: pp. 169–170; *OS* 2: p. 15: . . . nous esperons qu'on la trouvera saincte et pure: veu qu'elle est simplement reiglee à l'edification, dont nous avons parlé.

[101] Blankenburg, *Church Music,* p. 517.

[102] *Ibid.* Italics added.

[103] Erroneously attributed in the 1542 edition to Psalm 159 [sic].

be kept abreast of his thinking on the subject, and so the additional passage on singing in church which he prepared for the *Institution* of 1543 is, as it were, a Latin counterpart to the French *Epistle* as well as a significant amplification of part of its contents. Indeed, he must surely have been thinking of the latter while he was writing it, for in its overall structure the addition follows precisely the same triadic pattern, historical, Scriptural, and Patristic, in its appeal first to the practice of the ancient church, then to the witness of Saint Paul, and finally to the *Confessions* of Saint Augustine.

That a close relationship between the two documents in fact existed in his mind is at once apparent from the opening sentence. "It is evident," Calvin writes, "that the practice of singing in church, to speak also of this in passing, is not only a very ancient one but also was in use among the apostles." [104] The statement simply rephrases his assertion in the *Epistle* that "this is not something invented a short time ago." Immediately thereafter he refers to Saint Paul, as he had also done in the *Epistle*, now, however, with a subtle but significant difference. As if to give the fullest possible weight to the Apostle's authority, he quotes him directly, something which, in this context, he had not done before.

This we may infer from Paul's words: "I will sing with the spirit and I will sing with the mind" [1 Cor. 14:15]. Likewise, Paul speaks to the Colossians: "Teaching and admonishing one another . . . in hymns, psalms, and spiritual songs, singing with thankfulness in your hearts to the Lord." [Col. 3:16 p.] For in the first passage he teaches that we should sing with voice and heart; in the second he commends spiritual songs, by which the godly may mutually edify one another. [105]

He turns then to Saint Augustine.

Calvin had told the council in the *Articles* that he wished the psalms "to be sung in the church as we have it from the example of the ancient church." The principal source for the statement at that time was no doubt Bucer. Calvin's extensive reading in Saint Augustine since then had considerably deepened his knowledge of that ancient church, however, and, as a result, he writes now, in effect, as a church historian, scrupulously clarifying and correcting the general statements he had made in 1537 and 1542. With respect to the use of the psalmody which he was defending, he owns to the fact that "Augustine testified that this practice was not universal when he states that the church of Milan first began to sing only under Ambrose . . . then the remaining Western churches followed Milan. For a little before he had said that this custom had come from the Eastern churches." [106] The source as well as the antiquity of the custom

thus authenticated by Augustine, Calvin proceeds to a discussion of the music to be sung. There is, he argues, a "gravity which is fitting in the sight of God and the angels," and to this "gravity" the singing must be "tempered." [107] The idea and the language are again those of the *Epistle*. The requirement for a uniquely sacred kind of music, characterized above all by gravity, derives fundamentally from the unique nature of the audience for which it is designed, and this music is not for the entertainment of men.

Calvin's concern for the unique quality of the music of his psalmody had been first expressed in the *Epistle*, where he had voiced it, significantly, within an Augustinian frame of reference. "There must always be concern," he had written, "that the song be neither light nor frivolous, but have gravity and majesty, as Saint Augustine says." Now, still with reference to Augustine, he shifts the focus of his concern from the nature of the music to the relationship between the music and the words in the singer. Even if the music is not merely entertaining, even if in fact it does achieve that unique quality to which it must always aspire, Calvin cautions nevertheless that "our ears be not more attentive to the melody than our minds to the spiritual meaning of the words." [108] Men must never lose sight of the words they are singing, and something of the urgency of this imperative for Calvin is suggested by his reference, immediately following, to the experience of Augustine. The latter had analyzed his multiple, ambiguous responses to the singing of psalms in the church in the tenth book of the *Confessions*. "Yet when it happens," he had admitted, "that I am more moved by the singing than by what is sung, I confess myself to have sinned wickedly, and then I would rather not have heard the singing." [109] He recalls what Athanasius had done, requiring "the readers of the psalm to use so slight an inflection of the voice that it was more like speaking than singing," and this he sometimes thought was "the safer way." [110] On the other hand he acknowledged "the great utility of this custom" when awareness, not of the singing but of the words, of "what is sung," was always uppermost in men's minds. [111] Calvin briefly summarized the passage, and simply recorded Augustine's approval of psalmody.

"Therefore," he continues, "when this moderation is maintained [*Hac ergo adhibita moderatione*], it [psalmody] is without any doubt a most holy and

---

[104] *Institutes*, p. 895; *OC* **II**: pp. 658–659; *OS* **4**: p. 341.

[105] *Institutes*, p. 895; *OC* **II**: p. 659; *OS* **4**: pp. 341–342.

[106] *Institutes*, p. 895; *OC* **II**: p. 659; *OS* **4**: p. 342.

[107] *Ibid*: Et certe si ad eam, quae Dei et Angelorum conspectum decet, gravitatem attemperatus sit cantus, . . .

[108] *Institutes*, p. 895; *OC* **II**: p. 659; *OS* **4**: p. 342.

[109] *Augustine: Confessions and Enchiridion*, newly translated and edited by Albert C. Outler, *The Library of Christian Classics* (London, SCM Press Ltd., 1955) 7: p. 231.

[110] *Ibid*.

[111] *Ibid*.

salutary practice." [112]   The words "this moderation," would seem at first to pose a problem, for moderation has not previously been mentioned.   Furthermore it appears preceded by the adjective "this," pointing obviously to some specific antecedent, but one which is not immediately clear from the text.   Calvin has been alluding to the *Confessions,* however, and there Augustine had approved psalmody *only* if for the singer the words took priority over the melodies.   In this sense the music was "moderated" to the text, and it is to this Augustinian moderation, unmentioned in the *Institution* but still very much in his mind, that Calvin refers.   The first responsibility of the singer is, as he had insisted earlier, "to the spiritual meaning of the words," not to the melody.   Necessarily, then, by way of concluding the addition, Calvin rejected "such songs as have been composed only for sweetness and delight of the ear" for they "are unbecoming to the majesty of the church and cannot but displease God in the highest degree." [113]

X.   THE ADDITION TO THE *EPISTLE*: 1543

The addition to the *Institution* had consisted of two parts: an exhibition of some of the Scriptural and Patristic evidence supporting the legitimacy of psalmody, and a discussion of the psalmody itself.   The historical evidence was unambiguous: clearly psalmody had been in use in the ancient church.   Consequently it should be restored to the worship of a church rightly and truly reformed in the sixteenth century.   The treatment of music, on the other hand, had been less completely affirmative.   The idea of moderation with which Calvin had brought the addition to its close was a critical one, implicitly raising fundamental questions about music itself as well as its relationship to words which Calvin evidently did not wish to treat in the *Institution.*   Indeed, as he himself said, he had introduced the matter of singing in church only "to speak also of this in passing [*ut id quoque obiter dicam*]," [114] and as a matter of fact the addition of 1543 was never thereafter altered or enlarged.   A more appropriate place to discuss his ideas and his concerns about music lay to hand in the *Epistle,* however, and to it, accordingly, Calvin returned, adding a long and eloquently argued essay [115] which is nothing less than an exploration of some of the major implications of the idea of moderation, [116]

and it is in this respect that the addition to the *Epistle* is fundamentally related to the passage in the *Institution.*   Furthermore, inasmuch as the idea of moderation with respect to psalmody is essentially Augustinian, the addition may also be read as an extended, although for the most part, indirect, gloss on the passage in the *Confessions* to which Calvin had referred only briefly in the *Institution.*

Yet another reason for the addition is to be found in its opening words: "And how much more widely the practice of singing may extend." [117]   Ever since his first insistence in the *Articles* of 1537 on the necessity for singing the psalms Calvin had concerned himself, when writing about music, only with its role in the public worship of the church.   This had been the case even in the *Epistle* of 1542.   Fully aware of its value in that regard, he acknowledges now that it may have equal value in private devotions, ". . . even in the homes and in the fields."   His point of view has significantly widened; in the addition of 1543 music may become *everywhere* "an incentive for us, and, as it were, an organ for praising God and lifting up our hearts to Him . . .," [118] and the possibility of this expansion of the role of music in the spiritual life of men leads Calvin to an analysis of its nature which in its scope and depth moves beyond anything he had written thus far.

He develops his ideas by continuing the sequence of antitheses begun in the text of 1542.   On the one hand "the Holy Spirit exhorts us so carefully through the Holy Scriptures to rejoice in God."   "All our joy," he says, "is there reduced, as it were, to its true end." [119]   On the other hand the condition of man is such that he rejoices rather in vanity.   Accordingly

[112] *Institutes,* p. 896; *OC* **II**: p. 659; *OS* **4**: p. 342.

[113] *Ibid.*

[114] *Institutes,* p. 895; *OC* **II**: p. 658; *OS* **4**: p. 341.

[115] *Cf.* Doumergue, *Calvin* **4**: p. 337: "Ces deux pages en effet étaient ce qu'il y avait de plus remarquable dans la préface, et elles constituaient un éloge du chant et de la musique tel qu'on a pu dire: Luther lui-même ne l'avait pas dépassé."

[116] See Léon Wencelius, "L'idée de modération dans la pensée de Calvin," *Evangelical Quarterly* **7** (1935): pp. 87–94 and 295–317; *ibid.,* **8** (1936): pp. 75–93 and 279–319.

[117] *OC* **VI**: pp. 169–170; *OS* **2**: p. 15: combien que l'usaige de la chanterie s'estende plus loing.   Oliver Strunk, *Source Readings in Music History. From Classical Antiquity through the Romantic Era* (New York, W. W. Norton and Company, Inc., 1950), pp. 345–348, gives a translation of the musical portions of the *Epistre au Lecteur,* but misplaces the point at which the addition of 1543 begins (p. 347, n.6).   The error is difficult to understand, for he based his translation on the text in *Oeuvres choisies de Jean Calvin.* Publiées par La Compagnie des Pasteurs de Genève (Genève, A. Jullien, 1909), pp. 169–176, where the beginning of the addition is correctly noted (p. 173, n. 1).

[118] *OC* **VI**: pp. 169–170; *OS* **2**: pp. 15–16: C'est que mesme par les maisons et par les champs ce nous soit une incitation et comme un organe à louer Dieu, et eslever noz cueurs à luy. . . .

[119] *OC* **VI**: pp. 169–170; *OS* **2**: p. 16: . . . le Sainct Esprit nous exhorte si soigneusement par les sainctes escritures, de nous resiouyr en Dieu, et que toute nostre ioye soit là reduite, comme à sa vraye fin.   For the idea of joy in Calvin, see Léon Wencelius, "L'idée de joie dans la pensée de Calvin," *Revue d'histoire et de philosophie religieuses* **15**, Nos. 1–2 (January-April, 1935): pp. 70–109.   For the special relationship of joy to music, see *idem., L'esthétique de Calvin* (Paris, Société d'édition "Les Belles Lettres," 1938), pp. 250–251, 257, 272–273, 293, and 295; *cf.* also Blankenburg, *Calvin,* col. 659.

"our Lord, to distract us and withdraw us from the temptations of the flesh and the world, presents us all means possible to occupy us in that spiritual joy which He recommends to us so much." [120] The importance which Calvin has now come to attach to music then becomes apparent, for of all the means which God has created to turn men toward that spiritual joy, "music is either the first or one of the principal." It is nothing less than "a gift of God deputed to that use." [121] The idea of utility,[122] so quintessentially Calvinian, appears here with particular force; music was given to men for the express purpose of "recreating man and giving him pleasure." It is "dedicated to our profit and welfare," [123] and precisely because music possesses these specific ends for which it was created, man must be all the more careful not to abuse it. He should therefore "moderate the use of music," by which in this context Calvin means to "serve everything virtuous." [124]

Another antithesis follows. Calvin is, on the one hand, convinced that music, if properly moderated, can raise men up to spiritual joy; were this not possible God would not have given it to men. He is just as convinced, on the other hand, that without moderation music can debase man, leading him to the "disordered delights [*delices desordonées*]" of

the world, indeed to any "obscenity [*impudicité*]." [125] So, for instance, in addition to general examples of the latter, he cites specifically the complaint of "the ancient doctors of the Church" about the "unseemly and obscene songs" which the people were then singing; they tended nothing less than to "the corruption of the world." [126] The judgment was not exaggerated, for with respect to music

there is scarcely anything in the world which is more capable of turning or moving this way and that the morals of men, as Plato prudently considered it. And in fact we experience that it has a secret and almost incredible power to arouse hearts in one way or another.[127]

To his personal experience of this power, to which he had earlier witnessed in the *Epistle* of 1542, he adds now, in conventional humanist fashion, the judgment

---

[120] *OC* **VI**: pp. 169–170; *OS* **2**: p. 16: . . . nostre Seigneur, pour nous distraire et retirer des allechemens de la chair et du monde, nous presente tous moyens qu'il est possible, afin de nous occuper en ceste ioye spirituelle laquelle il nous recommande tant.

[121] *Ibid*: Or entre les autres choses, qui sont propres pour recreer l'homme et luy donner volupté, la Musicque est, ou la premiere, ou l'une des principalles: et nous faut estimer que c'est un don de Dieu deputé à cest usaige.

[122] See especially "The Idea of Utility in the Thought of John Calvin (with a discussion by J. T. McNeill)" in E. Harris Harbison, *Christianity and History* (Princeton, New Jersey, Princeton University Press, 1964), pp. 249–269.

[123] *OC* **VI**: pp. 169–170; *OS* **2**: p. 16: . . . desdiée a nostre proffit et salut.

[124] *Ibid*: . . . à moderer l'usage de la musicque, pour la faire servir à toute honnesteté. . . . Lenselink, *De Nederlandse Psalmbereijmingen*, p. 160, suggests that Calvin is influenced here by Bucer's *Vorrede* to the *Strassburger Gesangbuch* of 1541 (*BDS* **7**: p. 579): . . . und also allweg in allen dingen allen lust, freud, begirde, reitzen und ermanen und was hiezu dienstlich und die gemüter zu bewegen, krefftig, als dan die Music fur andern dingen ist, zu Got unserm Vater gerichtet und gestellet haben, also, das kein Lied uberal, kein seitenspil anders dann von und zu christlichen geistlichen hendelen gesungen und gebrauchet wurde; *cf. ibid*., p. 578: . . . so solte die Music, alles gesang und seitenspil (welche vor anderen dingen das gemüt zu bewegen, hefftig und hitzig zu machen, mechtig sind) nirgend anders, dann zu gotlichem lob, gebet, lehre und ermanung gebrauchet werden.

[125] *OC* **VI**: pp. 169–170; *OS* **2**: p. 16: . . . qu'elle ne soit point occasion de nous lascher la bride à dissolution, ou de nous effeminer en delices desordonées, et qu'elle ne soit point instrument de la paillardise ne d'aucune impudicité.

[126] *Ibid*: Pour ceste cause, les Docteurs anciens de l'Eglise se complaignent souventesfois de ce que le peuple de leur temps estoit addonné à chansons deshonnestes et impudiques, lesquelles non sans cause ilz estiment et appellent poison mortelle et Satanique pour corrompre le monde.

[127] *Ibid*: Car à grand peine y a il en ce monde qui puisse plus tourner ou flechir cà et là les meurs des hommes, comme Plato l'a prudemment consydere. Et de fait nous experimentons qu'elle a une vertu secrette et quasi incredible à esmouvoir les cueurs en une sorte, ou en l'autre. *Cf.* Bucer's *Vorrede* (*BDS* **7**: p. 578): Demnach des menschen art und natur so gestaltet ist, das in zu allerlei anmutigkeit, es seien freude, leid, liebe, zorn, geistlich andacht, leichtfertige wildikeit und was der affect und beweglicheiten sind, nichs so gewaltig beweget, als artliche Musicgesang und seitenspil, aus warer kunst auf solche anmutigkeiten und affection gerichtet. Paul-André Gaillard, *Loys Bourgeoys, sa vie, son oeuvre comme pédagogue et compositeur. Essai biographique et critique suivi d'une bibliographie et d'un appendice* (Lausanne, Imprimeries Réunies S. A., 1948), pp. 30–31, suggests that Calvin is indebted to Luther at this point. He adduces the following passage: "Das einige kann ich jetzt anzeigen, welches auch die *Erfahrung* bezeuget, dass nach dem heiligen Wort Gottes nichts nicht so billig und so hoch zu rühmen und zu loben, als eben die Musica, nämlich aus der Ursach, dass sie aller *Bewegung des menschlichen Herzen* ein Regiererin, ihr mächtig und gewaltig ist, durch welche doch oftmals die Menschen, gleich als von ihrem Herrn, regieret und überwunden werden. Denn nichts auf Erden kräftiger ist, die Traurigen fröhlich, die Frölichen traurig, die Verzagten herzenhaftig zu machen, die Hoffärtigen zur Demut zu reitzen, die hitzige und übermässige Liebe zu stillen und dämpfen, den Neid und Hass zu mindern, —und wer kann alle Bewegung des menschlichen Herzen, welche die Leute regieren, und entweder zu *Tugend oder zu Laster* reitzen und treiben, erzählen?" Here, however, a similarity between Luther and Bucer is more evident than between either of them and Calvin. Furthermore the power of music was a *topos* so universally acknowledged in the history of Western European thought that with respect to it, unless two or more texts are exceptionally alike, the *direct* influence of one author on another should be discounted. In this instance it is more accurate to speak of *parallels* between all three Reformers.

of Plato.[128] Music is a source for good or evil, and in the antitheses in which this is implied—"this way and that," "in one way or another,"—Calvin reveals himself as standing squarely in the humanist tradition of the sixteenth century in which "faith in the elevating powers of music must perforce have its corollary in the fear of a corruptive influence which vulgar and cheap music would exercise."[129] What distinguishes Calvin from this tradition is the rigorous and consistently sustained use to which he put the notion of moderation *in practice*. The power of music is such that "we ought to be the more diligent in regulating it in such a way that it be useful to us and not at all pernicious,"[130] and in these, his own words, Calvin best described his regulating role as editor in the production of the Genevan Psalter.

What Calvin means by "music" has hitherto been unclear. So general has been his use of the word that one may conclude that by it perhaps he meant simply any kind of artistically ordered sound. But, he continues, "in speaking now of music, I understand two parts, that is to say the letter, or subject and matter; second, the song or the melody."[131] With this clarification his usage becomes explicit: in the remainder of the addition music always means singing, that is to say a combination of words and music.

Now the fact that it is a *combination* of the two poses a very nearly insoluble problem:

It is true that every evil word (as Saint Paul says) perverts good morals, but when the melody is with it, it pierces the heart that much more strongly and enters into it; just as through a funnel wine is poured into a container, so also venom and corruption are distilled to the depth of the heart by the melody.[132]

At no other time does Calvin so emphasize the daemonic nature of music as he does here. He had begun the addition to the *Epistle* by asserting that music was a gift of God. Shortly thereafter he had vented his concern for its capacity to alter men's moral disposition or change their hearts. Now he denounces it for its power to enhance and intensify evil words. Naturally these are to be feared when spoken, but when accompanied by melody they penetrate men's hearts far more deeply and destructively. This being the case, should not music, as Calvin understands it here, be eliminated from worship entirely? On the other hand, if melody could so greatly magnify the impact of evil words, could it not perform a like function with good words? And if so, was not then the question of the words to be sung more crucial than ever? That is precisely the conclusion toward which Calvin has been so carefully and so consciously aiming: *the text, in fact, is all-important*. "What is there then to do?" he asks, and confidently replies: sing the Psalms of David. If one accepts the proposition of Saint Augustine, as Calvin does, that "no one is able to sing things worthy of God unless he has received them from Him,"[133] then the most exhaustive search[134] will yield "no better

---

sinne ligt, erst durchs gesang noch anmutiger und tieffer in sinne und hertz gestecket wurt. The similarity between the two passages (which escaped the attention of Lenselink) is so striking that Calvin's indebtedness to Bucer at this point would seem virtually assured. But, as has been pointed out by H. G. Koenigsberger, Calvin's sentence is "pure Plato, even to the metaphor of the funnel"; see "Music and Religion in Modern European History," his brilliant contribution to *The Diversity of History. Essays in honour of Sir Herbert Butterfield*, edited by J. H. Elliott and H. G. Koenigsberger (London, Routledge and Kegan Paul, 1970), pp. 35–78 at p. 44. The passage in Plato cited by Koenigsberger (pp. 39–40) is *The Republic III*, 411: "And, when a man allows music to play upon him and to pour into his soul through the funnel of his ears those sweet and soft and melancholy airs of which we were just now speaking, and his whole life is passed in warbling and the delights of song; in the first stage of the process the passion or spirit which is in him is tempered like iron, and made useful, instead of brittle and useless. But, if he carries on the softening and soothing process, in the next stage he begins to melt and waste, until he has wasted away his spirit and cut out the sinews of his soul; and he becomes a feeble warrior." *The Dialogues of Plato* translated by B. Jowett (Oxford and London, 1892), 3rd Edition, III, p. 99. *Cf.* H. P. Clive, "The Calvinist Attitude to Music, and its Literary Aspects and Sources," *Bibliothèque d'Humanisme et Renaissance* 19 (1957), No. 1: pp. 80–102; No. 2: pp. 294–319; and especially, on the sources, 20 (1958): pp. 79–107.

[133] *OC* **VI**: pp. 169–172; *OS* 2: p. 17: Or ce que dit S. Augustin est vray, que nul ne peut chanter choses dignes de Dieu, sinon qu'il ait receu d'iceluy. . . .

[134] *Ibid*: . . . parquoy quand nous aurons bien circuy par tout pour cercher cà et là. . . . The phrase may perhaps be autobiographical. While at Strasbourg Calvin was exposed to the wide variety of texts used in the liturgy there, and after three years of testing, as it were, the efficacy of both non-

---

[128] For the influence of Plato and Neo-Platonism on Western musical thought, see now the fine summary in Robert M. Isherwood, *Music in the Service of the King. France in the Seventeenth Century* (Ithaca and London, Cornell University Press, 1937), pp. 1–54.

[129] Frederick W. Sternfeld, "Music in the Schools of the Reformation," *Musica Disciplina* 2 (1948): pp. 99–122 at p. 103.

[130] *OC* **VI**: pp. 169–170; *OS* 2: p. 16: Parquoy nous devons estre d'autant plus diligens à la reigler, en telle sorte qu'elle nous soit utile et nullement pernicieuse.

[131] *OC* **VI**: pp. 169–170; *OS* 2, pp. 16–17: Or en parlant maintenant de la Musicque, ie comprens deux parties, asçavoir la lettre, ou subiect et matiere. Secondement le chant, ou la melodie.

[132] *OC* **VI**: pp. 169–170; *OS* 2: p. 17: Il est vray que toute parolle mauvaise (comme dit sainct Paul) pervertit les bonnes meurs, mais quand la melodie est avec, cela transperce beaucoup plus fort le cueur et entre au dedans tellement que comme par un entonnoir le vin est iecté dedans le vaisseau, aussi le venin et la corruption est distillé iusques au profond du cueur, par la melodie. *Cf.* Bucer's *Vorrede* (*BDS* 7, 579): Daher es auch erschröcklich ist, zu gedencken, was ergernis bei der juget und anderen durch die teufelischen bullieder angestifftet wurt, so das, welches on das zu fil anmutig und im

songs nor more appropriate to the purpose than the Psalms of David which the Holy Spirit made and spoke through him." [135] The words, far from being evil, are demonstrably good and cannot be otherwise for they are of divine origin. Moreover, men are assured of this fact, for "when we sing them, we are certain that God puts the words in our mouths, as if He Himself were singing in us to exalt His glory." [136] The problem posed by the fact that music is a *combination* of words and music is thus solved because the problem of the text is solved. The psalms will serve as a talisman against the power of music, and melody, with all its capacity for intensification, will now accompany words which are made and spoken by the Holy Spirit, even by God Himself, with the result that men will have

songs not only seemly, but also holy, which will be like spurs to incite us to pray to and praise God, to meditate on His works in order to love, fear, honor, and glorify Him.[137]

The solution reached in theory, Calvin proceeds to urge the universal adoption of the psalms to the exclusion of all other songs.

Only let the world be so well advised that in place of songs in part empty and frivolous, in part stupid and dull, in part obscene and vile, and in consequence evil and harmful, which it has used up to now, it may accustom itself hereafter to singing these divine and celestial hymns with the good King David.[138]

The real climax of the *Epistle* of 1542, although sited in the last sentence but one, was Calvin's unqualified distinction between the music which men make "at table and in their homes" and the music for the psalms. The substance of the sentence here, likewise penultimate within the addition, is clearly an elaboration, framed in the most uncompromising language, of that earlier distinction between the secular and the sacred. Calvin's first concern in 1542 had been for the music; now it is for the text, a shift in

emphasis for which Augustine's *Confessions* must be largely responsible. Consequently the antithesis between the songs which the world "has used up to now" and the psalms is as much the real climax of the addition of 1543 as was the antithesis between music for entertainment and music for worship formulated in 1542. The parallelism, too striking to be accidental, illuminates nicely the structural relationship as well as the continuity of argument which Calvin saw between the two documents.

XI. THE UNIQUENESS OF THE PSALMS

On a deeper and more significant level of interpretation, however, that final, powerfully fashioned antithesis also marks the climax of the development of Calvin's theology of music in the years between the *Institution* of 1536 and the addition to the *Epistle* of 1543. Hesitant at first to admit music to worship, later granting to psalmody an indispensable place in the liturgy, Calvin proposes now that even outside the liturgy only the psalms be sung.

The distance he had traveled in reaching this conclusion is intimated in the memorandum which he submitted to the synod of Zürich in May in 1538. Early in August of the preceding year Messieurs of Bern had been requested officially to abolish from their territories the practice of singing lascivious *rondes* while dancing.[139] Evidently in this they had had some success, for the concluding *Article* of the memorandum reads as follows:

XIV. Finally, inasmuch as our Bernese friends provide precedent with respect to lascivious and obscene ditties and the dances which have always been associated with their rhythms, we would request that they [the Genevan government] eliminate such filth from their domain also. . . .[140]

The statement is forthright and concise. Calvin sought the prohibition from Geneva of certain songs, in this instance those specifically obscene and associated with dancing. Moreover his request was immediately preceded by the *Article* in which he reiterated his insistence on the introduction of psalmody into the public worship of the city. But between the prohibition of obscene songs on the one hand, and the practice of psalmody on the other, there was then no demonstrable connection.

Four years later, however, a relationship between the two had clearly emerged in his mind. In the little preface to the first French liturgy for Strasbourg (1542), Calvin informs the reader that in it the

---

Scriptural sacred and spiritual songs and vernacular versions of the psalms, he was confirmed in his decision, reached in 1537, to restrict his congregational psalmody to the latter.

[135] *OC* **VI**: pp. 171–172; *OS* 2: p. 17: . . . nous ne trouverons meilleures chansons ne plus propres pour ce faire, que les Pseaumes de David: lesquelz le sainct Esprit luy a dictz et faitz.

[136] *Ibid*: Et pourtant, quand nous les chantons, nous sommes certains que Dieu nous met en la bouche les parolles, comme si luy-mesmes chantoit en nous pour exalter sa gloire.

[137] *OC* **VI**: pp. 169–170; *OS* 2: p. 17: . . . c'est d'avoir chansons non seulement honnestes, mais aussi sainctes: lesquelles nous soyent comme esguillons pour nous inciter à prier et louer Dieu, à mediter ses oeuvres, afin de l'aymer, craindre, honnorer et glorifier.

[138] *OC* **VI**: pp. 171–172; *OS* 2: pp. 17–18: . . . seullement que le monde soit si bien advisé qu'au lieu de chansons en partie vaines et frivolles, en partie sottes et lourdes, en partie salles et vilaines, et par consequent mauvaises et nuysibles, dont il a usé par cy devant, il s'accoustume cy apres à chanter ces divins et celestes Cantiques avec le bon Roy David.

[139] Herminjard, **V**: p. 6, n. 17.

[140] *OC* **X**², No. 111: p. 192; Herminjard, **V**, No. 708: p. 6: Postremo, quum in lascivis et obscoenis cantilenis ac choraeis quae ad illarum numeros semper sunt compositae, nostri Bernatium exemplum praetexant, oratos volumus, ut e sua quoque ditone tales spurcitias eliminent. . . . I am especially grateful to Professor F. L. Battles, who translated the passage at my request for this essay.

psalms have been published with their melodies ". . . so that you will have seemly songs instructing you in the love and fear of God in place of [*au lieu de*] those which are commonly sung which are concerned only with dissipation and all [kinds of] vice." [141] Here musical versions of the psalms are offered as substitutes for obscene songs, whether associated with dancing or not. The emphasis, to be sure, is still on the obscene, but the way is not far to the concluding assertion of the addition of 1543 that the psalms should replace all existing songs, whether obscene or not. The power of music attached to such worldly texts is such that "we ought to be the more diligent in regulating it in such a way that it be useful to us and not at all pernicious," Calvin had said, and in this decision for the psalms *alone* the idea of regulation is pushed to its logical conclusion. The distinction between the secular and the sacred which Calvin had been at such pains to establish in 1542 is to be obliterated, for he looks now to the eventual elimination of all secular vocal music. In the ideal future, when men and women sang, not only at public worship, but in their private prayers and everywhere else, even in their entertainment "at table and in their homes," they would sing only the "divine and celestial hymns" of David.

In this vast design the influence of Bucer is once again to be detected. It must not be forgotten that Calvin had been on the most intimate terms with him for the three years which he spent in Strasbourg. They shared an interest in music, and had ample opportunity as well to discuss it. Consequently, when in 1541 Bucer set forth his ideas on the role of music in worship and the world in the *Foreword* to the *Strasbourg Song Book,* Calvin, although unable to read the German in which they were formulated, would nonetheless have been thoroughly conversant with them. By then Bucer, too, had moved well beyond the positions which he had defended in the *Justification and Demonstration from Holy Scripture* of 1524 and the *Tetrapolitan Confession* of 1530. Writing eleven years later in the *Foreword,* he had now come to the radical conclusion that all music, instrumental as well as vocal, should be employed exclusively in the service of religion.

Thus music, all singing and playing (which above all things are capable of mixing our spirits powerfully and ardently), should be used in no other way except for sacred praise, prayer, teaching, and admonition . . . so that absolutely no song and no instrumentalizing may be sung or used except by and for Christian spiritual activities.[142]

Grounded on that first principle, Bucer envisioned a program for the sacralization of music which would proceed, as it were, in two parallel stages.

If the only proper use of music in general was religious, and if, more concretely, song had to be directed exclusively to "Christian spiritual activities," then one of the two stages was clearly the elimination of all secular songs. This should be done as soon as possible, for in so important a matter as music, given its unique power, there was no time to be lost. Accordingly, Bucer directed a passionate exhortation to all Christians generally, regardless of their professions, "whoever would or could" to

give counsel and assistance so that such lascivious, devilish, ruinous songs will be cast out and destroyed, and the holy Psalms and sacred songs be made pleasing to all Christians, young and old alike, and brought into steady use, particularly among the leaders and servants of the Churches.[143]

The other stage, no less pressing, was the musical education of children. In the context of the *Foreword* these were Bucer's special concern, although by no means to the exclusion of others. Only the next generation could be raised exclusively on psalms and spiritual songs; by the same token only the next generation could be carefully and constantly insulated against the evils of secular song. Their training in this regard was crucial to the success of the program. To their teachers, therefore, Bucer addressed himself at the close of the *Foreword,* urging them to: "turn their efforts toward teaching the children such holy, sacred songs faithfully, and accustoming them to sing the same, and not allow them either to hear or to sing any frivolous, worldly, and wanton songs." [144]

---

und seitenspil (welche vor anderen dingen das gemut zu bewegen, hefftig und hitzig zu machen, mechtig sind) nirgend anders, dann zu gotlichem lob, gebet, lehre und ermanung gebrauchet werden . . . also, das kein Lied uberal, kein seitenspil anders dann von und zu christlichen geistlichen hendelen gesungen und gebrauchet wurde.

[143] *BDS* **7**: pp. 579–580: Darumb, wer da kondte oder mochte, der solt dazu rahten und helffen, das solche uppige teufelische, verderbliche gesang abgethan und verspulget würden und die heiligen Psalmen und gotselige lieder allen Christen, jungen und alten gemein, lustig gemacht und in stetig ubung bracht wurden. Und zum furnemisten die Fursteher und Diener der Kirchen.

[144] *BDS* **7**: p. 582: Und die, so die kinder leren . . . fleis ankern, das sie die kinder solich heilige gotliche Lieder getrewlich leren, auch die selbigen zu singen anhalten und alle

---

[141] *OS* **2**: p. 12: Affin que tu eusse chansons honnestes t'enseignantes l'amour et crainte de dieu, au lieu de celles que communement on chante qui ne sont que de paillardise et toute villenie.

[142] *BDS* **7**: pp. 578–579: . . . so solte die Music, alles gesang

While writing the 1542 text of the *Epistle to the Reader,* Calvin's whole attention had been focused on the problem of finding an appropriate music for the psalms; it was at that time that he made the decision for the sacred style. His concern was for the public worship of the church, so that his thinking on psalmody then was musical and liturgical. The movement of his thought on the subject away from questions both of musical style and the shape of the liturgy is suggested by the preface to the Genevan liturgy of 1542. Not until the addition to the *Epistle* of 1543, however, does this new direction become explicit and central. The text of the latter, saving its final sentence, is devoted entirely to a consideration of psalmody as a spiritual aid to the daily life of Christians apart from their formal worship, and only in that larger, extra-liturgical context, precisely that of Bucer's *Foreword,* did Calvin disclose his long-held familiarity with Bucer's program.

What he took from it was not the idea that all music should be put only to religious use, for he does not specifically allude to instrumental music. It was, rather, Bucer's proposal that all secular songs be eliminated and replaced by religious ones; with this sweeping substitution Calvin clearly was in essential agreement. He adopted it, however, with one profoundly significant qualification. Bucer had spoken throughout the *Foreword* of psalms *and* sacred songs or spiritual songs, and in doing so, as he himself more than once acknowledged, he was following the tradition established by Luther of permitting all kinds of music and all kinds of texts to be sung in church as well as outside it. But what was variety for Luther and Bucer was promiscuity for Calvin. The psalms alone were sacred; and for their singing he intended, if possible, to have one, and only one, sacred style. For God and His angels as well now as for the world below, nothing else was, or even could be, appropriate, and with that decision Calvin's valuation of vernacular psalmody had reached its apogee.

XII. THE SINGING OF THE PSALMS

He turns next to a consideration of how the psalms should be sung, summarizing briefly his three fundamental requirements for their proper performance.

There was, first of all, the total commitment of the heart. In the *Institution* of 1536 Calvin had warned "that unless voice and song, if interposed in prayer, spring from deep feeling of heart, neither has any value or profit in the least with God." His proposal in 1537 to introduce psalmody into the worship of the Genevan church was grounded on his conviction that it would be edifying only if it were, quite literally, heartfelt. In 1543 he reaffirms what he had written

eight years earlier when, for the first time, he had raised the question of worship music. "It is necessary for us to remember what Saint Paul says, that spiritual songs can be sung truly only from the heart." [145] From that basic condition, as it were, Calvin had not deviated, nor would he at any time in the future.

But to the heart he joins now intelligence. Inasmuch as the whole thrust of the *Epistle* had been his insistence that the worshipper understand at every point what was said and done, the second requirement is inevitable; it was, in fact, explicit in his insistence on the use of the vernacular in public worship in the 1536 *Institution.* Of considerably greater significance is the fact that Calvin's stress on the necessity for intelligence in singing is made here within a specifically Augustinian frame of reference. "Now the heart requires intelligence," he writes,

and in that (says Saint Augustine) lies the difference between the singing of men and that of the birds. For a linnet, a nightingale, a parrot may sing well, but it will be without understanding. Now the peculiar gift of man is to sing knowing what he is saying.[146]

So persuasive indeed is Augustine's influence at this point that Calvin even reverses his initial priority, putting the intelligence before "the heart and the affection."

Memory, the third requirement for the proper singing of psalms, is by no means least; indeed it is a peculiarly indispensable one, for the efficacy of the intelligence and the heart in turn depend on the fact that "we have the hymn imprinted on our memory." [147] If music and text both are already familiar, then neither can serve to distract the worshipper, and he is in a very real sense freed from any immediate concern for them. Calvin intends thereby to make the two-fold movement from mind to mouth and heart to

---

o   o   e
leichtfertige weltliche bulerische lieder ihnen weder zu horen
o
noch zu singen gestatten.

[145] *OC* **VI**: pp. 171–172; *OS* **2**: p. 17: Au reste, il nous faut souvenir de ce que dit S. Paul, que les chansons spirituelles ne se peuvent bien chanter que de cueur.

[146] *Ibid*: Or le cueur requiert l'intelligence. Et en cela (dit sainct Augustin) gist la différence entre le chant des hommes et celuy des oyseaux. Car une Linote, un Roussignol, un Papegay, chanteront bien, mais ce sera sans entendre. Or le propre don de l'homme est de chanter, sachant qu'il dit: ... Paul-André Gaillard, *op. cit., supra,* n. 127, p. 31, suggests that at this point Calvin is once more influenced by the following passage from Luther: "In den unvernünftigen Thieren aber, Saitenspielen und andern Instrumenten, da höret man allein den Gesang, Laut und Klang, ohne Red und Wort; dem Menschen aber ist allein, vor den andern Creaturen, die Stimme mit der Rede gegeben, dass er sollt können und wissen, Gott mit Gesängen und Worten zugleich zu loben, nämlich mit dem hellen klingenden Predigen, und rühmen von Gottes Güte und Gnade, darinnen schöne Wort und lieblicher Klang zugleich würde gehöret." It is more likely, however, that both Reformers are indebted here to Augustine.

[147] *OC* **VI**: pp. 171–172; *OS* **2**: p. 17: ... apres l'intelligence doit suivre le cueur et l'affection, ce qui ne peut estre que nous n'ayons le cantique imprimé en nostre memoire. ...

mouth as spontaneous and uncomplicated, in the exactest sense of the word, as possible, so that melody, intensifying the good words of the psalms, may be used that much more effectively in praying to God or praising Him. If this ideal is realized in practice, then we shall never "cease from singing."[148] The phrase, far from being hyperbolic, provides yet another striking indication of the extent of the development of Calvin's attitude toward music since 1536. In the first *Institution*, discussing the silent, private prayer of the individual, he had laid paramount stress on the Pauline injunction to "pray without ceasing." The addition of words or music to this constant prayer was worthless unless these came "from deep feeling of heart." By 1543 he had become so convinced of the efficacy of music to engage the heart, and thereby to enhance prayer, public as well as private, that "to pray without ceasing" was at the same time "never to cease from singing." The association between the two had become indissoluble in his mind.

Finally, in the last sentence of the addition, Calvin returns to the question of the music. "Touching the melody," he writes, "it has seemed best that it be moderated in the manner *which we have adopted*."[149] The phrase underscored suggests that already Calvin had found and approved a sacred style, one which in his judgment conformed to that ideal of a "gravity and majesty appropriate to the subject [*convenable au subiect*]" on which he had insisted in the *Epistle* of 1542 and the addition to the *Institution* of 1543. Moreover the manner adopted is suitable, not simply for singing in private prayers and elsewhere apart from formal worship, but even "for singing in the Church."[150] And with the adoption of that style, Calvin's work on the Genevan Psalter had begun.

XIII. CONCLUSION

The succeeding editions of the Psalter gave unwavering expression to a theology of music which had been maturing in Calvin's mind between 1536 and 1543. In the development of its salient features three distinct stages may be identified, and to a consideration of these we must now turn.

Its initial formulation is to be found indisputably in the *Articles* of 1537. There Calvin made known for the first time his decision to introduce vernacular congregational psalmody into the liturgy of Geneva. Against the background of the passages on music and worship in the *Institution* of 1536, so unequivocal an announcement was to a certain degree unexpected.

But when he wrote the *Articles,* Calvin was no longer the scholar writing in seclusion. He was, to the contrary, actively engaged in the business of reform, and the conditions of public worship had assumed for him an immediacy which they had not had before, and which in conscience he could not now evade. What he had witnessed during his first months in Geneva clearly displeased him; his language on that score leaves no doubt whatsoever. "Certainly at present," he wrote, "the prayers of the faithful are so cold that we should be greatly ashamed and confused." For such an emotionally impoverished worship the essential remedy, as Calvin understood it, was the addition of music, specifically singing the psalms. His theology of music thus arises from, and is conditioned by, his intense desire for what was, in effect, a transformation of the experience of worship. When the citizens of Geneva prayed together in public, Calvin wanted above all to engage their hearts, for there lay the source of true prayer. That "emotion of the heart within" had somehow to be "aroused and stimulated," and he had come to the conclusion that of all the means available and appropriate, psalmody could best accomplish the engagement which he envisioned.

It could not be wrought, however, could not even be initiated, unless the people understood what they were singing, and so the psalms were to be translated into their language. Unlike Luther in this regard, who would retain Latin as a liturgical language and use German as well,[151] the vernacular was for Calvin indispensable for public worship, and to its exclusive use he had in fact committed himself even before drawing up the *Articles,* for in the chapter on prayer in the *Institution* of 1536 he had argued that

public prayers must be couched not in Greek among the Latins, nor in Latin among the French or English (as has heretofore been the custom) but in the language of the people, which can be generally understood by the whole assembly. For this ought to be done for the edification of the whole church, which receives no benefit whatever from a sound not understood.[152]

And just as the psalms were to be understood by the whole church, so, too, was the whole church to sing them. Again unlike Luther, Calvin would have no specially trained choirs set apart from the rest of the congregation.[153] The latter had to learn the music at

---

[148] *Ibid*: . . . pour ne iamais cesser de chanter.

[149] *OC* **VI**: pp. 171–172; *OS* **2**: p. 18: Touchant de la melodie, il a semblé advis le meilleur qu'elle fust moderée, en la sorte que nous l'avons mise pour emporter poidz et maiesté convenable au subiect. . . .

[150] *Ibid*: . . . et mesme pour estre propre à chanter en l'Eglise. . . .

[151] *Cf.* Blankenburg, *Calvin,* col. 662: Auch hierin unterscheidet sich Calvin von Luther, der bekanntlich nebeneinander deutsche und lat. Gottesdienstordnungen geschaffen hat, während für Calvin die lat. Kultsprache zu den Missbräuchen der ma. Kirche gehört.

[152] *Institution,* p. 101; *OC* **I**: p. 88; *OS* **1**: p. 103.

[153] *Cf.* Blankenburg, *Calvin,* col. 662: Somit wird Luthers grosse Tat, den Gemeindegesang zum tragenden Faktor des Gottesdienstes erhoben zu haben, im calvinistischen Gottesdienst noch ausschliesslicher durchgeführt. See also Söhngen, *Calvin,* p. 51: Weit energischer noch als Luther hat Calvin dafür Sorge getragen, dass die ganze Gemeinde mit dem Singen ihre evangelische "Mündigkeit" bezeugte; . . .

first from the children, to be sure, but eventually everyone was to know the music and participate in the singing. Calvin's construction here of what may be called the congregational principle was thus strict: the hearts of all, without exception, were to be engaged in similar fashion by music.

It was this understanding of vernacular congregational psalmody that Calvin brought to Strasbourg, and it was there that he grasped its efficacy to the full. The "ardor" in singing the psalms which he encountered in his congregation was the determining factor behind his Strasbourg Psalter of 1539. And when he returned to Geneva in 1541 it was his desire to translate that "ardent" worship to the city of "cold prayers" which inspired the Genevan Psalter of 1542. Thus from its inception Calvin's theology of music in its liturgical dimension was *pastoral*; it was an articulation of his life-long concern, as practical as it was profound, for the edification and intensification of the worship experience of each and every member of his congregation. The Psalter was conceived, and always would be considered by him, as an indispensable instrument for the realization of his ideal of true prayer.

In the *Articles* of 1537, the *Epistle to the Reader* of 1542, and the addition to the *Institution* of 1543 Calvin had justified vernacular congregation psalmody in part by citing the example of the early church. It was Bucer who had directed his attention to the fact that the singing of psalms had been practiced in "the first and apostolic churches," and Bucer's repeated appeal to history struck a responsive chord in Calvin. His legal as well as his humanistic studies had meant an immersion in the world of antiquity; his sense of history, classical and Christian, was profound, and the image of the ancient church was never far from his mind. Indeed, the order of worship which he drew up for the Genevan church in 1542 was specifically "according to the custom of the ancient Church." Thus from its inception Calvin's theology of music in its liturgical dimension was also *historical*. The Psalter was conceived, and always would be considered by him, as an indispensable instrument in his life-long attempt to restore to Christianity the authentic and unadulterated worship of the ancient church.

The necessity for the use of vernacular psalmody in public worship definitively established, Calvin turned next to the question of the music itself. He came to the decision, doubtless while in Strasbourg, that when the psalms were sung they should have, quite literally, their *own* music. They should be rendered, as it were, in a style so distinctive that when heard it would be set apart at once and unmistakably from all other existing music, ecclesiastical as well as secular, and associated exclusively with the psalms. In this noble ideal of a *musica sacra* he parted company decisively with Luther and Bucer, and in its realization he was to be successful, for the melodies of the Genevan Psalter in its completed form are, in fact, with one exception, both new and different. Calvin sought and eventually won a uniquely "new song."

From Saint Augustine came the inspiration for its three constitutive elements, namely the twin qualities of gravity and majesty, and the necessity for moderating or tempering the music to the text. The music for the sacred style could not be "composed only for sweetness and delight of the ear"; to do so would accord to music an independent standing which was impermissible. The text had first priority always, and melodies had to be created, therefore, which were at all times "appropriate to the subject [*convenable au subiect*]." In this sense, then, music had always to be subservient to the text, intensifying every word by means of the peculiar gravity and majesty of its style, so that uppermost in men's minds while singing was not the music, but the words, "what is sung." The condition is that of Saint Augustine as expressed in the *Confessions;* only on these terms would he admit singing to the church, and to this insistence on the priority of the text Calvin subscribed without reservation. Thus in its musical dimension, that is to say in its stylistic ideal of gravity and majesty and its consistent subordination of the music to the text, Calvin's theology of music was expressly, and, in the exactest sense of the word, essentially *Augustinian*.

The third and final stage was marked by Calvin's decision to replace all existing secular songs with musical versions of the psalms. The new dimension to his thinking, stimulated by Bucer, was that of the moral status of words and music. The *Foreword* to the *Strasbourg Song Book* had stressed over and over again the fearful distance between the psalms and sacred and spiritual songs on the one hand, and on the other "the lascivious, injurious, alluring and other worldly songs, including the poison leading to all vices and evil which they leave behind."[154] Against these Bucer had railed, deploring their destructive effects, especially on the young. The problem of contemporary song as he understood it was fully as much a social as it was a musical one. At issue was the welfare of the community, and the threat to its moral health posed by these songs was so great that nothing less than their total elimination was required. By 1543 Calvin had come to share Bucer's concern; as he acknowledged in the addition to the *Epistle,* "unseemly and obscene songs" could, in fact, corrupt the world. Music could degrade men and destroy them,

---

[154] *BDS* 7: p. 581: . . . die upige, schandliche bul-und andere weltlieder sampt dem gifft, das sie zu allen lasteren und bosen sitten hinder inen lassen, . . .

especially when associated with evil words. Not-withstanding the fact that it was a gift of God, its very existence was dangerous, for almost nothing else in all creation was so "capable of turning or moving this way and that the morals of men, as Plato prudently considered it." It had, then, to be regulated so diligently that it would serve only what was virtuous, and to that end, therefore, Calvin concluded that only the psalms should be sung and these only in a sacred style, removed as far as possible from any worldly connotations.

The immediate initiative for the decision came from Bucer. Calvin's allusion to Plato, however, points to the larger context in which that decision was taken, for "Plato's theory of the difference between good and bad or, rather, moral and immoral music . . . celebrated its greatest triumphs in the sixteenth century." [155] Belief in the distinction between the two on his authority was central to humanist discourse on music throughout the century, and the addition to the *Epistle,* as well as Bucer's *Foreword,* fall within, and belong to, this Platonic tradition. Thus in its social dimension, in its concern for the morality of music and text, Calvin's theology of music was *humanistic.* The Psalter was designed to restrain the power of music on a world-wide scale, and so focus it that music could and would move men's morals and hearts not "this way and that" or "in one way or another," but in one direction only, namely toward "everything virtuous."

All four dimensions, pastoral, historical, Augustinian, and humanistic ultimately are fused, however, and made indissolubly one in Scripture. When Calvin proposed to re-order the whole vocal-musical life of the Christian community around the singing of the psalms, it was because the words of the psalms were God's words, put by God in the mouths of the singers, just as He had put them first in the mouth of David. To sing "these divine and celestial hymns" was to witness to the Word, and "if one looks at the matter properly, it is solely the Biblical Word at its base which legitimizes music in public worship" [156] as well as private devotions. Calvin's vernacular psalmody in the last analysis is nothing other than a formulation, in uniquely musical terms, of the Reformation principle of *sola scriptura.* Thus from its inception Calvin's theology of music in its textual dimension was *Scriptural.* The Psalter was conceived, and always would be considered by him, as an indispensable instrument for the prosecution of his ministry of the Word of God to the city of Geneva and the wider world beyond.

---

[155] H. G. Koenigsberger, *op. cit., supra,* n. 132, p. 40.

[156] Söhngen, *Calvin,* p. 52: . . . ja, recht besehen, ist es allein das zugrundeliegende Bibelwort, das die Musik im Gottesdienst legitimiert.

APPENDIX
I
FOREWORD

Martinus Bucer, servant of the Word of the Churches in Strasburg, wishes all Christian believers Grace and Peace from God the Father and our Lord Jesus Christ.[1]

It is acknowledged by all who read the Holy Bible that from the beginning the pious and truly believing custom has been to proclaim God's praise with singing, and in doing so, to give voice to the great pleasure, delight, and joy with which their [i.e., the singers] hearts were filled to bursting in and from God, so full, moreover, that they could no longer contain within themselves such pleasure, delight, and joy. Thus their listeners would also be attracted to, reminded of, and made happy by the acknowledgment of, and thankfulness for, God and His goodness. Likewise, they have used song for their pious lamentations, prayers, proclamations, teachings, prophesyings, and admonitions, for in their actions they have poured forth absolutely truly, earnestly, and reverently their lamentation, prayer, proclamation, teaching, prophesying, and admonition, always from hearts full to overflowing. And they have always desired right earnestly to bring their godly attitude into the hearts of others, and to make them [i.e., others] desirous and eager for the same.

For this purpose the music and song ordained by God is not only completely joyful and charming, but also marvelous and powerful. The nature and temperament of man is so formed that nothing moves it so powerfully to all sorts of moods—be they joy, sorrow, love, anger, spiritual reverence, giddy abandon, and whatever other emotions and affections there are—than artful musical singing and playing directed with skill at such moods and affections. Add to this whatever especially concerns men and gladdens them —whatever they like to think about most, with whatever they wish always to be involved, and to which they therefore gladly direct their efforts so that these things will also be made known and pleasant as much to themselves as others—regarding such actions they wish immediately to make songs. In this way these things will not only be spoken of, but sung, and thereby everything will be brought into the hearts of the people all the more thoroughly.

For we who are the old dear friends of God—even the more dear since God the Father has enabled us to know His son our Lord Jesus Christ so much more— there is nothing which should penetrate our hearts more deeply, and be the only thing with which we are concerned, than the sacred: how we might properly acknowledge, love, praise, and exalt Him, our

---

[1] The translation of Bucer's *Vorrede* is made from the text in *BDS* 7: pp. 577–582.

Creator and Father, through Jesus Christ our Lord and Redeemer. And for this purpose many things arouse and affect us. Thus music, all singing and playing (which above all things are capable of moving our spirits powerfully and ardently), should be used in no other way except for sacred praise, prayer, teaching, and admonition.

We should love God with all our hearts, all our souls, and all our strength. Now if we had such love, we would really do as Saint Paul teaches, 1 Cor. X [31] and Coloss. III [17]: whether we eat or drink, or whatever we begin and take up in words or works, we would begin, take up, and do everything in the name of our Lord Jesus Christ to the praise of God, saying thanks to God the Father through Him our Lord. And therefore always in all things—all pleasure, joy, desires, affections, and admonitions and whatever is serviceable for this and capable of moving the spirit—music, as in other things, has been placed before and directed to God our Father, so that absolutely no song and no instrumentalizing may be sung and used except by and for Christian spiritual activities.

If one can rejoice and enjoy oneself with such holy, sacred songs—add to which the fact that they make us noticeably better—then in such endeavors one can have only real joy and happiness. For otherwise no good understanding, and therefore more gall than honey (as someone says) is found, where otherwise there is a God and understanding. Where, then, there is no God and no understanding, there is literally eternal Hell, even if one does not now perceive it as such, and one goes on living in a storm, singing and dancing and behaving absurdly.

Now, however, the evil one has brought matters to such a pass (which is greatly to be deplored) that music, this wonderful art and gift of God, is misused for lasciviousness. This is therefore not only a grievous sin insofar as the art is a magnificent gift of God, but also insofar as it intensifies more powerfully, penetrating the heart and bringing into the spirit that [lasciviousness] for which it is being used. Accordingly it is horrible to contemplate what unpleasantness is stirred up among the young and others by devilish, seductive songs, so that whatever without song is too charming and lies in the senses, is insinuated by song more charmingly and deeper into the senses and the heart.

If we must give an accounting to God of every thoughtless word, as in all conscience we must, what, then, shall happen to those who in a headstrong manner through song ensnare their heart and thoughts in such injurious poems and songs. And woe to all who see and hear in this description their children, household, and whomsoever they must protect. But here one sees, sadly, what sort of Christians these people are, and (as the proverb has it) every bird will be known by his song, and the word of the Lord will be fulfilled: with whatever the heart is full, the mouth comes forth.

Therefore whoever could or would should give counsel and assistance so that such lascivious, devilish, ruinous songs will be cast out and destroyed, and the holy Psalms and sacred songs made pleasing to all Christians, young and old alike, and brought into steady use, particularly among the leaders and servants of the Churches.

Therefore Dr. Martin Luther sometime ago had published some Psalms and spiritual songs composed by himself—as he is in such matters highly gifted, as indeed also in everything that may strengthen the true knowledge of Christ, and be serviceable and ameliorating for true Christian activity and administration of the Churches—with some other highly placed servants of Christ, also particularly gifted in this matter, and brought them before the congregations of Christ. The same has happened here and in many other Churches, but only in little books which each Christian uses individually in Churches and elsewhere.

But now when some congregations of Christians began to prepare common large hymnbooks, particularly for the young, so that they might better win and keep the measured and unison song in the sacred congregations, some people were of a mind to pay highly for the making of these books. The honored printer, Jörg Waldmüller, called Messerschmid, to further the good in the dear Churches and to promote sacred song in Christian congregations, schools, and places of learning, was requested and commissioned to print a songbook with no little cost and trouble. He bent every effort, as the work itself shows, with the result that the Psalms and spiritual songs included herein might be published as clearly as possible and corrected to the best of knowledge. Now since this work is directed at the many Churches which do not have the same song [i.e., music] in use, many Psalms and spiritual songs are furnished here with music so that each Church may find herein those [songs] which it is accustomed to use. Thus you will find herein first of all nearly all those which Dr. Martin Luther published in his book at Wittenberg; afterwards the best ones which we are accustomed to sing here at Strasburg and in other Churches known to us.

But since, as Dr. Luther justifiably complains, among the appropriately pleasing and spiritual songs by him and others many unnecessary and unspiritual and unedifying are mixed—and also among those which already have some style and can be edifying, and even in this there is a great difference—the name of the poet is placed under each Psalm and spiritual song so that one may recognize who has created each poem and work and thereby no one will be accredited with what is not his.

This faithful and useful service should be received gratefully by the congregations and all those who are Christians, inasmuch as by means of it the general improvement of the kingdom of Christ is sought. And although some Psalms and spiritual songs are definitely better in art and spiritual nature than others (among them are all those which Dr. Martin Luther has composed), there is nothing printed in this book which does not follow sacred Word, and is not serviceable for the enhancement of piety. Accordingly, no one should object that the printer, his publisher, and adviser have gathered together here so many Psalms and spiritual songs in order to serve so many Churches.

The Lord should see to it that all leaders and servants of the Churches, together with all Christians, exert their best efforts to ensure that among the young as well as the whole congregation of Christ such beautiful Christian songs come into use and practice, so that when there is an assembly, or the people sing among themselves, they will be joyful with such Psalms and songs as are published here and there alike (as all the saints of the Old and New Testament were accustomed to do, and as Saint Paul admonishes). By these means, then, our souls will be drawn towards, instructed in, and educated to God our Creator and Christ our Saviour, and to all other discipline, edification, Christian love, and friendship, and will be led on to cast out and destroy the lascivious, injurious, alluring, and other worldly songs, including the poison leading to all vices and evil which they leave behind.

It is even now the time in which whoever embraces God should do so in all seriousness; God does not like us half-hearted. The long deserved anger of God presses strong against us. The warnings of God increase daily, and punishments keep step with them. Woe to us if we do not wake up, if we do not look more deeply into ourselves, and become more zealous in Christian action.

Therefore fathers and mothers should remember to whom they have given and offered their children in baptism, and remember that they are answerable not to these only, and not to their own flesh and blood only, but also to God's children. And those who teach children should remember what a precious treasure is entrusted to them, sons and daughters of the Most High, whom the dear angels serve. And since this age has a preference for singing, and wishes to be led to the good in joyful ways, they should turn their efforts toward teaching the children such holy, sacred songs faithfully, and accustoming them to sing the same, and not allow them either to hear or to sing any frivolous, worldly, and wanton songs. For, as Saint Paul teaches, not only should no injurious and bad, but also no foolish and flippant things be heard or occur among us, such as things which do not pertain to our calling, but count as vain thanksgiving. But rather praise and exalt God, so that through us His holy name may be ever more sanctified, His kingdom widened, and His will truly and more joyfully lived. Amen.

II

EPISTLE TO THE READER [2]

As it is a thing rightly required by Christianity, and one of the most necessary, that each of the faithful observe and maintain the communion of the Church in his neighborhood, attending the assemblies which are held on Sunday as well as on other days to honor and serve God, so is it also expedient and reasonable that everyone know and understand what is said and done in the temple in order to receive benefit and edification from it. For our Lord did not institute the order which we are bound to observe when we gather together in His name merely to amuse the world by a spectacle, but rather desired that from it profit would come to all His people as Saint Paul testifies, commanding that everything which is done in the Church be directed to the common edification of all, something which the servant would not have commanded had it not been the intention of the Master. Now this cannot be done unless we are taught to understand everything which has been ordained for our use. For to say that we can have devotion, either at prayer or at ceremony, without understanding anything about them, is a gross delusion, no matter how much it is commonly said. A good affection toward God is a thing neither lifeless nor bestial, but is a quickening movement proceeding from the Holy Spirit when the heart is truly touched and the understanding enlightened. And in fact, if one could be edified by things which one sees without understanding what they mean, Saint Paul would not so vehemently forbid speaking in an unknown tongue, and would not use the argument that there is no edification unless there is doctrine. Nevertheless, if we wish truly to honor the holy ordinances of our Lord which we use in the Church, the most important thing is to know what they contain, what they mean, and to what purpose they tend, in order that their observance may be useful and salutary, and in consequence rightly regulated.

Now there are in sum three things which our Lord has commanded us to observe in our spiritual assemblies, namely, the preaching of His Word, the public and solemn prayers, and the administration of His sacraments. I refrain from speaking of preaching at this time inasmuch as it is not in question. Touching the two other parts which remain, we have the express commandment of the Holy Spirit that prayers

---

[2] The translation of Calvin's *Epistre au Lecteur* is made from the text in *OS* **2**: pp. 12–18; *cf. OC* **VI**: pp. 165–172.

be made in the common language and understood by the people. And the Apostle says that the people cannot respond, Amen, to the prayer which has been made in an unknown tongue. Now since prayer is made in the name of all and on behalf of all, everyone should be a participant. Wherefore this has been a very great affront to those who have introduced the Latin language into the Churches where it is not commonly understood. And there is neither subtlety nor sophistry which can excuse them from this custom which is perverse and displeasing to God. For one must not presume that He will be agreeable to what is done directly contrary to His will, and, as it were, in defiance of Him. Nor can one any longer defy Him, acting thus against His prohibition, and glorying in this rebellion as if it were a thing holy and very praiseworthy.

As for the sacraments, if we look truly at their nature, we recognize that it is a perverse custom to celebrate them in such a way that the people have nothing but the spectacle, without explanation of the mysteries which are contained in them. For if these are visible words, as Saint Augustine calls them, they must not be merely an exterior spectacle, but doctrine must be joined to them to give them understanding. And so our Lord, in instituting them, expressly demonstrated this, for He says that they are testimonies of the alliance which He made with us, and which He confirmed by His death. It is certainly necessary, then, in order to accord them their proper place, that we know and understand what is said in them. Otherwise it would be in vain that our Lord opened His mouth to speak if there were no ears to hear. And this is not a subject for lengthy disputation, for when the matter is judged with a sober disposition, there is no one who will not admit that it is pure trickery to amuse the people with signs whose meaning has not been explained to them. Wherefore it is easy to see that one profanes the sacraments of JESUS Christ administering them in such a manner that the people do not understand the words which are spoken in them. And in fact one sees the superstitions which issue from this. For it is commonly agreed that the consecration, as much of the water at Baptism as of the bread and the wine in the Supper of our Lord, are like a kind of magic; that is to say, that when one has opened one's mouth and pronounced the words, insensible creatures feel the effect, yet men understand nothing. Now the true consecration is that which is made by the word of faith when it is declared and received, as Saint Augustine says. This is expressly realized in the words of JESUS Christ, for He does not say to the bread that it should become His body, but He directs His word to the company of the faithful, saying: Take, eat, and so forth. If we wish, then, rightly to celebrate the sacrament, it is necessary for us to have the doctrine

by which what is signified in it is declared to us. I know perfectly well that that seems like an outrageous opinion to those who are unaccustomed to it, as is the case with all new things. But it is certainly right, if we are disciples of JESUS Christ, that we prefer His institution to our practice. And what He instituted from the beginning ought not to appear to us like novel opinion.

If that still cannot penetrate everyone's understanding, it will be necessary for us to pray to God that it please Him to enlighten the ignorant, to make them understand how much wiser He is than any man on earth, so that they will learn to be satisfied no longer with their own judgment or with their foolish wisdom, and be enraged with their leaders who are blind. Meanwhile, for the use of our Church, it seemed well advised to us to have published a formulary of prayers and the sacraments in order that everyone might know what he should say and do in the Christian assembly. The book will be profitable not only for the people of this Church, but also for all those who wish to know what form the faithful should maintain and follow when they gather together in the name of JESUS Christ. We have therefore collected as in a summary the manner of celebrating the sacraments and sanctifying marriage; likewise the prayers and praises which we use. We will speak a little later of the sacraments.

As for the public prayers, there are two kinds: the ones made with the word only, the others with song. And this is not a thing invented a short time ago. For from the first origin of the Church, this has been so, as appears from the histories. And even Saint Paul speaks not only of praying by mouth, but also of singing. And in truth we know from experience that song has great force and vigor to arouse and inflame the hearts of men to invoke and praise God with a more vehement and ardent zeal. There must always be concern that the song be neither light nor frivolous, but have gravity and majesty, as Saint Augustine says. And thus there is a great difference between the music which one makes to entertain men at table and in their homes, and the psalms which are sung in the Church in the presence of God and His angels. Now when anyone wishes to judge correctly of the form which is here presented, we hope that he will find it holy and pure, seeing that it is simply directed to the edification of which we have spoken.[3]

And how much more widely the practice of singing may extend. It is even in the homes and in the fields an incentive for us, and, as it were, an organ for praising God and lifting up our hearts to Him, to console us by meditating on His virtue, goodness, wisdom, and justice, something which is more necessary than one can say. For in the first place it is not

---

[3] At this point the text of 1542 ends; what follows is the addition written in 1543.

without cause that the Holy Spirit exhorts us so carefully through the Holy Scriptures to rejoice in God, and that all our joy is there reduced, as it were, to its true end. For He knows how much we are inclined to rejoice in vanity. As thus then our nature draws us and induces us to look for all manner of demented and vicious rejoicing, so to the contrary our Lord, to distract us and withdraw us from the temptations of the flesh and the world, presents us all means possible to occupy us in that spiritual joy which He recommends to us so much. Now among the other things which are appropriate for recreating man and giving him pleasure, music is either the first or one of the principal, and we must value it as a gift of God deputed to that use. Wherefore that much more ought we to take care not to abuse it, for fear of fouling and contaminating it, converting it to our condemnation, when it was dedicated to our profit and welfare. If there were no other consideration than this alone, it ought indeed to move us to moderate the use of music, to make it serve everything virtuous, and that it ought not to give occasion for our giving free rein to licentiousness, or for our making ourselves effeminate in disordered delights, and that it ought not to become an instrument of dissipation or of any obscenity. But there is still more. For there is scarcely anything in the world which is more capable of turning or moving this way and that the morals of men, as Plato prudently considered it. And in fact we experience that it has a secret and almost incredible power to arouse hearts in one way or another.

Wherefore we ought to be the more diligent in regulating it in such a way that it be useful to us and not at all pernicious. For this reason the ancient doctors of the Church complain frequently of the fact that the people of their times were addicted to unseemly and obscene songs which not without reason they judge and call mortal and Satanic poison for the corruption of the world. Moreover, in speaking now of music, I understand two parts, that is to say the letter, or subject and matter; second, the song or the melody. It is true that every evil word (as Saint Paul says) perverts good morals, but when the melody is with it, it pierces the heart that much more strongly and enters into it; just as through a funnel wine is poured into a container, so also venom and corruption are distilled to the depth of the heart by the melody. What is there then to do? It is to have songs not only seemly, but also holy, which will be like spurs to incite us to pray to and praise God, to meditate on His works in order to love, fear, honor, and glorify Him. Now what Saint Augustine says is true, that no one is able to sing things worthy of God unless he has received them from Him. Wherefore, when we have looked thoroughly everywhere and searched high and low, we shall find no better songs nor more appropriate to the purpose than the Psalms of David which the Holy Spirit made and spoke through him. And furthermore, when we sing them, we are certain that God puts the words in our mouths, as if He Himself were singing in us to exalt His glory. Wherefore Chrysostom exhorts men as well as women and little children to accustom themselves to sing them, in order that this may be, as it were, a meditation for associating themselves with the company of angels. As for the rest, it is necessary for us to remember what Saint Paul says, that spiritual songs can be sung truly only from the heart. Now the heart requires intelligence, and in that (says Saint Augustine) lies the difference between the singing of men and that of the birds. For a linnet, a nightingale, a parrot may sing well, but it will be without understanding. Now the peculiar gift of man is to sing knowing what he is saying. After the intelligence must follow the heart and the affection which is impossible unless we have the hymn imprinted on our memory in order never to cease from singing.

For these reasons the present book, even for this cause, in addition to the rest which has been said, ought to be under exceptional consideration by everyone who desires to enjoy himself in seemly fashion and in accordance with God, to look to his welfare and to the profit of his neighbors. And so there is no necessity to be particularly recommended by me, seeing that it carries its own value and praise. Only let the world be so well advised that in place of songs in part empty and frivolous, in part stupid and dull, in part obscene and vile, and in consequence evil and harmful, which it has used up to now, it may accustom itself hereafter to singing these divine and celestial hymns with the good King David. Touching the melody, it has seemed best that it be moderated in the manner which we have adopted to carry gravity and majesty appropriate to the subject, and even to be suitable for singing in the Church, in accordance with what has been said.

Geneva, 10 June 1543

BIBLIOGRAPHY

PRIMARY SOURCES

AUGUSTINE, SAINT. 1955. *Augustine: Confessions and Enchiridion* (newly translated and edited by Albert C. Outler, London).

BUCER, MARTIN. 1960– . *Deutsche Schriften* (5 v., edited by Robert Stupperich, Gütersloh).

——. Cypris, Ottomar Frederick. 1971. *Basic Principles: Translation and Commentary of Martin Bucer's Grund und Ursach, 1524* (University Microfilms, Michigan).

CALVIN, JOHN. 1863–1900. *Ioannis Calvini Opera Quae Supersunt Omnia* (58 v., edited by W. Baum, E. Cunitz, and E. Reuss, Brunswick).

——. 1919. *Aulcuns pseaulmes et cantiques mys en chant a Strasburg 1539* (Réimpression phototypographique précédée d'un avant-propos par D. Delétra, Geneva).

——. 1926–1936. *Joannis Calvini Opera Selecta* (5 v., edited by Peter Barth, Dora Scheuner, and Wilhelm Niesel, Munich).

——. 1954. *Calvin: Theological Treatises* (translated with introductions and notes by J. K. S. Reid, Philadelphia).

——. 1959. LA FORME DES PRIERES ET CHANTZ ECCLESIASTIQUES, auec la manière d'administrer les Sacremens et consacrer le Mariage: selon la coustume de l'Eglise ancienne (facsimile edition, Bâle).

——. 1960. *Calvin: Institutes of the Christian Religion* (2 v., edited by John T. McNeill and translated by Ford Lewis Battles, Philadelphia).

——. 1969a. *John Calvin: Six Metrical Psalms. An English Translation by Ford Lewis Battles Set to the Original Melodies of the Strassburg Psalter of 1539 As Harmonized by Sir Richard R. Terry* [*1932*] (Pittsburgh).

——. Battles, Ford Lewis. 1969b. *The Piety of John Calvin. An Anthology Illustrative of the Spirituality of the Reformer of Geneva* (Pittsburgh).

——. 1975. *Institution of the Christian Religion* (translated and annotated by Ford Lewis Battles, Atlanta).

FAREL, GUILLAUME. 1859. *La Manière et fasson quon tient es lieux que Dieu de sa grâce a visités* (Strasbourg/Paris).

——. 1867. *Le Sommaire de Guillaume Farel* (Geneva).

——. 1935. *Sommaire et Briefve Declaration* (Paris).

HERMINJARD, AIMÉ-LOUIS. 1866–1897. *Correspondance des réformateurs dans les pays de langue française, recueillie et publiée avec d'autres lettres relatives a la réforme et des notes historiques et biographiques* (Geneva).

SECONDARY SOURCES

BANNARD, YORKE. 1919. "Calvin as Musical Reformer." *The Monthly Musical Record* 49: pp. 151–152.

BLANKENBURG, WALTER. 1952. "Calvin." *Die Musik in Geschichte und Gegenwart* 2: cols. 653–666.

BLUME, FRIEDRICH. 1974. *Protestant Church Music, A History* (New York).

BOVET, FÉLIX. 1872. *Histoire du psautier des églises réformées* (Neuchatel).

BOYD, DOROTHY. 1950. "Calvin's Preface to the French Metrical Psalms." *Evangelical Quarterly* 22: pp. 249–254.

BUISSON, FERDINAND. 1892. *Sébastien Castellion, sa vie et son œuvre (1515–1563). Étude sur les origines du protestantisme libéral français* (2 v., Paris).

BÜSSER, FRITZ. 1949. "Calvin und die Kirchenmusik." *Musik und Gottesdienst* 3: pp. 97–106.

CHOISY, EUGÈNE. 1930. "Farel A Genève avec Calvin, De 1536 A 1538." *Guillaume Farel 1489–1565. Biographie nouvelle écrite d'après les documents originaux par un groupe d'historiens, professeurs et pasteurs de Suisse, de France et d'Italie* (Neuchatel/Paris), pp. 348–361.

CLIVE, H. P. 1957–1958. "The Calvinist Attitude to Music, and its Literary Aspects and Sources." *Bibliothèque d'Humanisme et Renaissance* 19: pp. 80–102, 294–319; 20: pp. 79–107.

DOUEN, ORENTIN. 1878–1879. *Clément Marot et le psautier huguenot* (2 v., Paris).

DOUMERGUE, ÉMILE. 1899–1927. *Jean Calvin, les hommes et les choses de son temps* (7 v., Lausanne/Paris).

——. 1909. "Music in the Work of Calvin." *The Princeton Theological Review* 7: pp. 529–552.

DUFOUR, THÉOPHILE. 1970. *Notice bibliographique sur le Catéchisme et la Confession de Foi de Calvin (1537) et sur les autres livres imprimés à Genève et à Neuchâtel dans les premiers temps de la réforme (1533–1540)* (Geneva).

ERICHSON, ALFRED. 1886. *L'Église française de Strasbourg au seizième siècle d'après des documents inedits* (Strasbourg).

GAILLARD, PAUL-ANDRÉ. 1948. *Loys Bourgeoys, sa vie, son œuvre comme pédagogue et compositeur. Essai biographique et critique suivi d'une bibliographie et d'un appendice* (Lausanne).

GARSIDE, CHARLES, JR. 1951. "Calvin's Preface to the Psalter: A Re-Appraisal." *The Musical Quarterly* 37: pp. 566–577.

——. 1966. *Zwingli and the Arts* (New Haven).

——. 1967. "Some Attitudes of the Major Reformers toward the Role of Music in the Liturgy." *McCormick Quarterly* 21: pp. 151–168.

GRAU, MARTA. 1917. *Calvins Stellung zur Kunst* (Wurzburg).

HARBISON, E. HARRIS. 1964. "The Idea of Utility in the Thought of John Calvin (with a discussion by J. T. McNeill)." *Christianity and History* (Princteon), pp. 249–269.

HASPER, H. 1955. *Calvijns beginsel voor de zang in de eredienst. Verklaard uit de Heilige Schrift en uit de geschiedenis der kerk. Een kerkhistorisch en hymnologisch onderzoek* (The Hague).

ISHERWOOD, ROBERT M. 1973. *Music in the Service of the King. France in the Seventeenth Century* (Ithaca).

JENNY, MARKUS. 1956. "Untersuchungen zu den Aulcuns Pseaumes (sic) et Cantiques mys en chant a Strasbourg 1539." *Jahrbuch für Liturgik und Hymnologie* 2: pp. 109–110.

KAMPSCHULTE, F. W. 1972. *Johann Calvin, seine Kirche und sein Staat in Genf* (Geneva).

KOENIGSBERGER, H. G. 1970. "Music and Religion in Modern European History." *The Diversity of History. Essays in honour of Sir Herbert Butterfield*, edited by J. H. Elliott and H. G. Koenigsberger (London), pp. 35–78.

LENSELINK, SAMUEL JAN. 1959. *De Nederlandse Psalmbereijmingen van de Souterliedekens tot Datheen, met hun voorgangers in Duitsland en Frankrijk* (Assen).

——. 1969. *Les Psaumes de Clément Marot* (Assen).

OLD, HUGHES OLIPHANT. 1975. *The Patristic Roots of Reformed Worship* (Zürich).

PANNIER, JACQUES. 1931. *Recherches sur la formation intellectuelle de Calvin* (Paris).

PARKER, T. H. L. 1975. *John Calvin: A Biography* (Philadelphia).

PIDOUX, PIERRE. 1962. *Le Psautier Huguenot du XVIᵉ Siècle. Mélodies et Documents* (2 v., Bâle).

REID, W. STANFORD. 1971. "The Battle Hymns of the Lord: Calvinist Psalmody of the Sixteenth Century." *Sixteenth Century Essays and Studies*, edited by Carl S. Meyer, 2: pp. 36–54.

REYBURN, HUGH Y. 1914. *John Calvin. His Life, Letters, and Work* (London).

ROGET, AMÉDÉE. 1870–1883. *Histoire du peuple de Genève depuis la Réforme jusqu'à l'Escalade* (7 v., Geneva).

SCHEUNER, DORA. 1950. "Calvins Genfer Liturgie und seine Strassburger Liturgie textgeschichtlich dargestellt." *Das Wort sie sollen lassen stahn, Festschrift für D. Albert Schädelin* (Bern), pp. 79–85.

SMITS, LUCHESIUS. 1957–1958. *Saint Augustin dans l'œuvre de Jean Calvin* (2 v., Assen).

SÖHNGEN, OSKAR. 1961. "Calvin" in "Theologische Grundlagen der Kirchenmusik." *Leiturgia. Handbuch des evangelischen Gottesdienstes* (Kassel) 4: pp. 38–62.

STERNFELD, FREDERICK W. 1948. "Music in the Schools of the Reformation." *Musica Disciplina* 2: pp. 99–122.

STRUNK, OLIVER. 1950. *Source Readings in Music History. From Classical Antiquity through the Romantic Era* (New York).

TERRY, SIR RICHARD RUNCIMAN. 1932. *Calvin's First Psalter* [*1539*] (London).

VUILLEUMIER, HENRI. 1927–1933. *Histoire de l'église ré-*

formée du Pays de Vaud sous le régime bernois (4 v., Lausanne).

WALKER, WILLISTON. 1909. *John Calvin, The Organizer of Reformed Protestantism: 1509–1564* (New York).

WENCELIUS, LÉON. 1935. "L'idée de joie dans la pensée de Calvin." *Revue d'histoire et de philosophie religieuses* **15**: pp. 70–109.

——. 1935–1936. "L'idée de modération dans la pensée de Calvin." *Evangelical Quarterly* **7**: pp. 87–94, 295–317; **8**: pp. 75–93, 279–319.

——. 1938. *L'esthétique de Calvin* (Paris).

WILL, ROBERT. 1938. "La première liturgie de Calvin." *Revue d'histoire et de philosophie religieuses* **18**: pp. 523–529.

ZAHN, ADOLPH. 1889. "Calvin als Dichter." *Zeitschrift für kirchliche Wissenschaft und kirchliches Leben* **10**: pp. 315–319.

INDEX

TO TEXT ONLY

MEMOIRS

OF THE

AMERICAN PHILOSOPHICAL SOCIETY

TRANSACTIONS

OF THE

AMERICAN PHILOSOPHICAL SOCIETY

The Invention of the Telescope. ALBERT VAN HELDEN.
Vol. 67, pt. 4, 67 pp., 4 figs., 1977. $6.00.

Spanish Red: An Ethnogeographic Study of Cochineal and the Opuntia Cactus. R. A. DONKIN.
Vol. 67, pt. 5, 84 pp., 12 figs., 9 maps, 1977. $7.00.

Soviet Civil Procedure: History and Analysis. DON W. CHENOWETH
Vol. 67, pt. 6, 55 pp., 1977. $6.00.

The Pioneer Stage of Railroad Electrification. CARL W. CONDIT.
Vol. 67, pt. 7, 45 pp., 17 figs., 1977. $6.00.

The Activists: Kurt Hiller and the Politics of Action on the German Left, 1914–1933. LEWIS D. WURGAFT.
Vol. 67, pt. 8, 114 pp., 1977. $12.00.

Crowner's Quest. THOMAS R. FORBES.
Vol. 68, pt. 1, 52 pp., 4 figs., 1978. $6.00.

Power, Authority, and the Origins of American Denominational Order: The Churches in the Delaware Valley, 1680–1730. JON BUTLER.
Vol. 68, pt. 2, 85 pp., 1978. $8.00.

The Sculpture of Giovanni and Bartolomeo Bon and their Workshop. ANNE MARKHAM SCHULZ.
Vol. 68, pt. 3, 81 pp., 77 figs., 1978. $6.00.

The Science of Minerals in the Age of Jefferson. JOHN C. GREENE AND JOHN G. BURKE.
Vol. 68, pt. 4, 113 pp., 2 figs., 1978. $10.00.

The City-Building Process: Housing and Services in New Milwaukee Neighborhoods 1880–1910. ROGER D. SIMON.
Vol. 68, pt. 5, 64 pp., 34 figs., 12 maps. 1978. $8.00.

French Secondary Education 1763–1790: The Secularization of ex-Jesuit Colleges. CHARLES R. BAILEY.
Vol. 68, pt. 6, 124 pp. 1978. $10.00

France and the Arab Middle East, 1914–1920. JAN KARL TANENBAUM.
Vol. 68, pt. 7, 50 pp., 1 map. 1978. $6.00.

The Transformation of the British Liberal Party: A Study of the Tactics of the Liberal Opposition. JOHN P. ROSSI
Vol. 68, pt. 8, 133 pp. 1978. $8.00.

A Translation of Vitruvius and Copies of Late Antique Drawings in Buonaccorso Ghiberti's *Zibaldone*. GUSTINA SCAGLIA.
Vol. 69, pt. 1, 30 pp., 13 figs. 1979. $6.00.

Evolution of the Plio-Pleistocene African Suidae. J. M. HARRIS AND T. D. WHITE.
Vol. 69, pt. 2, 128 pp., 135 figs., 18 plates. 1979. $12.00.

The Foundations of English Bankruptcy: Statutes and Commissions in the Early Modern Period. W. J. JONES
Vol. 69, pt. 3, 63 pp. 1979. $8.00.